A FORGOTTEN HERO

A FORGOTTEN HERO

FOLKE BERNADOTTE,
the Swedish Humanitarian
Who Rescued 30,000 People from the Nazis

Shelley Emling

Cover design: Michel Vrana
Author photo: © Scott Norvell

LIBRARY AND ARCHIVES CANADA
CATALOGUING IN PUBLICATION

Emling, Shelley, author
   A forgotten hero : Folke Bernadotte, the
Swedish humanitarian who rescued 30,000 people
from the Nazis / Shelley Emling.

Issued in print and electronic formats.
ISBN 978-1-77041-449-5 (hardcover)
ISBN 978-1-77305-309-7 (PDF)
ISBN 978-1-77305-308-0 (ePUB)

1. Bernadotte, Folke, 1895–1948. 2. Diplomats —
Sweden — Biography. 3. Philanthropists — Sweden
— Biography. 4. Holocaust, Jewish (1939–1945).
5. World War, 1939–1945 — Jews — Rescue
— Germany. 6. World War, 1939–1945 —
Concentration camps — Germany. 7. Biographies.
I. Title.

DL870.B47E45 2019   940.53'1835092
C2018-905325-9   C2018-905326-7

PRINTED AND BOUND IN CANADA   PRINTING: FRIESENS   5   4   3   2   1

For Scott, who always believes in me.

*And for Livia Frankel and all Holocaust survivors
who continue to speak out on behalf of the millions
who can no longer speak for themselves.
I am in awe of your resilience and your dedication
to educating younger generations about the horrors
that transpired. We can never forget.*

CONTENTS

"We weren't brought into this world to be happy, but to make others happy."

— FOLKE BERNADOTTE

How Could This Happen?

Manya Moszkowicz's life began to unravel on the first Friday in September of 1939.

Up until then, the chief discomforts the precocious 13-year-old faced in her small town in central Poland were physical — scrapes from running barefoot through fields of prickly vegetation, or a stomach upset by eating too many green apples. For her, there was no harbinger of the sinister events to come, the anti-Semitism already endemic in Central Europe at the time, even when she and her family moved to a larger city nearer the German border in 1938. She had noticed a few signs popped up around town urging Poles to boycott the hundreds of Jewish businesses scattered throughout Sosnowiec's streets. But Manya, a spindly girl with a round face, pretty dark eyes, and frizzy black hair, was rarely personally troubled by such intolerance.

On that late-summer morning in September, however, word spread that the Germans had invaded her country. By the end of the weekend, the Nazi armed forces, the

Wehrmacht, had rolled into town with their machine guns and shredded the only Polish soldier left in the vicinity to defend it. Overnight, Manya's world — and that of her parents and two brothers — was turned upside down. The wolf was on her doorstep. Anti-Semitism now wore a uniform and carried a weapon. Surely, she remembers thinking to herself, the world will not allow this miscarriage of justice to continue. Surely, the world powers will step in and stop the madman behind it all. Surely, someone will do something.

They did not.

In Sosnowiec, the anti-Semitic slurs and slights turned into outright terrorization. Jewish shop owners were jailed and their businesses handed over to German or Polish citizens. Authorities confiscated the valuables of Jewish families — right down to their bicycles and clocks — and distributed ration cards that allotted them only a miserly few staples. Jews were ordered to identify themselves by wearing white arm bands, which gave the Germans license to stop them in the streets and search for contraband. The local synagogue was burned to the ground while its congregation was forced to watch. German soldiers and civilians filmed themselves gleefully tormenting Jewish men in the streets, beating them or making them perform for the rolling cameras like dancing monkeys.

"From that day on, there was not a peaceful moment. Any insignificant thing meant life or death," Manya remembered some 70 years later. "Our entire life depended on the attitude of the SS or the Gestapo, or their degree of drunkenness."

One evening in particular stands out in her memory. A German had moved into an apartment in their building and demanded flower boxes for his balcony like those that adorned Manya's home. He barged through their front door, drunk and brandishing a pistol, along with the building's superintendent. Manya, her brothers, and their mother cowered in separate corners of the room while the belligerent man chased their father around the kitchen table shouting obscenities and waving the gun. Only when her father promised to deliver the flower boxes the next morning did the man agree to leave.

Surviving each day was a minor miracle. Neighbors vanished during the night, never to be seen or heard from again. A mandatory curfew led to indiscriminate arrests, often with the same outcome. The uncertainty was almost unbearable. Each evening, they would huddle in their parlor, waiting and praying, until each member of the family returned from the day's errands. Only after everyone was safe under one roof for the night would they heave a sigh of relief as an uneasy calm settled over the household. Day after day, it continued.

By the end of 1940, Jews from the surrounding towns and villages had been corralled in Sosnowiec, forced into ghettos where they could be controlled more easily. Thousands were deported daily, but thousands of others obtained jobs in local manufacturing shops dedicated to the war effort. In March 1941, Manya found such work, which afforded her a precious Sonderkarte, or proof of employment that had the power to prevent deportation. She worked as a seamstress sewing pockets on uniforms for Nazi soldiers and the mustard-brown shirts sported by the Hitler Youth. She labored doggedly and tried not to attract any attention, for fear she'd be sent away. And for many months, the routine continued without interruption.

But one evening two years later as her shift was ending, her luck ran out. SS officers surrounded the building and the entire staff was rounded up for deportation. She was immediately hustled off to a deportation center. Her parents were allowed to bring a single suitcase to her at the facility, but were forbidden from speaking to her. Manya stared into the faces of her parents as her younger brother clawed at the fence between them. They seemed to age 20 years in an instant.

"I assume each one of us had the same thought. Will we ever see each other again?" she recalled decades later. "As it turned out, that was the last time I saw my parents and my two brothers."

Days later, the rest of her family was sent off to the notorious Auschwitz Konzentrationslager, where they were immediately segregated. Manya's father and older brother were placed in one line while her mother and younger brother were placed in the other. Her father refused to be separated from his wife, so he and her brother crossed over to join her. It was an easy line to cut. It was destined for the gas chamber.

Manya was 17, and alone for the first time in her life.

She was sent to a new privately run camp in Gleiwitz that produced soot, or carbon black, for the rubber tires needed for the Nazi death machines rolling across Europe. The facilities were new, and clean, and she was assigned an office job. Others, not so lucky, toiled in dungeon-like chambers full of furnaces, where they breathed in noxious fumes as jet-black dust coated their clothes and any exposed parts of their perspiring bodies and faces.

Before long, the SS took over the camp, and it became an Auschwitz outpost. Her "jolly" (her word) German boss was replaced by stern SS officers and unforgiving female German overseers known as Kapos. The girls' heads were shaved, they were stripped of their clothes, and paraded into a room full of officers where every inch of their bodies was prodded and manhandled. Every orifice probed. For a modest young girl it was the ultimate humiliation.

"I cannot forget that feeling," she recalled later. "I don't think I got undressed to take a shower in front of my mother. And here, naked, we had to go in front of the Nazis to have our arms tattooed. And of course, from that day on, we were not called by our names but by our numbers. But believe me, they took away much more than our names."

Henceforth, Manya was known as 79357.

One evening in January 1945, as the Russian army ground down Adolf Hitler's army in the east, there was a commotion in the camp. They were being evacuated, Manya learned from her fellow prisoners. Those left behind, the whispers insinuated, were to be exterminated — put "through the Schornstein [chimneys]" in the vernacular of the SS officers — rather than left alive as evidence of the Nazi atrocities. Her close friend, Lola, lay nearly unconscious from fever in the infirmary, and Manya was faced with a choice: leave her friend to the fates or bring her on what was sure to be a perilous journey. She chose the latter.

Wearing the distinctive striped dresses and carrying only

a single blanket for protection from the January cold, Manya and her fellow prisoners made their way to the railroad station and waited for transport to another camp. After a night shivering in a barn, they were herded onto open-top rail cars normally used to transport coal for what they were told was a short journey. But the trip was nearly 600 kilometers — they were headed northwest to the Ravensbrück camp near Berlin.

The cars were packed. To prevent Lola from being crushed, Manya positioned her friend in a corner and clung to the side rails to brace herself against the mass of bodies pressing on her with each lurch of the car. For 10 days, the train rocked back and forth over narrow-gauge tracks through the bleak, war-scarred countryside — south at first, toward Czechoslovakia, in a desperate quest for a route unscathed by Allied bombs, then, finally, north again. Blankets soaked by falling and melting snow were their sole source of water. Their only nourishment was bread that sympathetic civilians hurled into the cars from overpasses. Czechs who came to the stations to offer sustenance to the starving women were pushed away and even fired at by Nazi guards. One woman, a nurse, who dared to raise her head above the side rails to ask a guard for water, was summarily shot and left to fall onto the tracks between the cars. Lola, by some miracle, survived the journey.

———

Manya, Lola, and the others could have had no way of knowing this, but the end of their nightmare was not far off. The most horrific war the world had ever seen was drawing to a close. By late 1944, the Allied vise had been tightening on the Third Reich, and the disintegration of the Nazi state was all but inevitable. In the west, Germany's desperate counter-offensive against the Allies in Belgium's Ardennes forest ended in complete failure, and in the east, the Red Army captured East Prussia and reached the Oder River, less than 50 miles from Berlin. Soon, the Third Reich consisted only of Germany proper, a few territories in central Europe, northern Italy, Denmark, Norway, and parts of Holland. The Nazi Air Force, the Luftwaffe, was a skeleton of an air fleet, and the Allies ruled Europe's skies, showering thousands of tons of bombs on Germany every day. The landscape through which the women were ferried looked almost lunar.

As Allied powers gained the upper hand, the world outside Germany began to breathe easier. But inside Germany, it was a different story. Adolf Hitler ignored or shrugged off the obvious, hurling orders in an increasingly erratic and delusional state. Backed into a corner, a dog is going to bite. And Hitler was nothing if not backed into a corner. Driven by an insane determination, he shunned every opportunity to surrender to whichever of the Allies might have received him most sympathetically. It mattered not that his cities were being reduced to rubble or that chaos reigned over his precious but shrinking Reich. The führer's hatred of the Jews only intensified. And he was not alone. Raging anti-Semitism remained rampant among his heel-clicking party officials and among a wide strata of the population at large.

Hitler declared that Germany would fight to the finish — until the very last man fell. Even by the horrifying standards set by years of Nazi genocide, the final phase of the war was to be more deadly, more vicious, more gruesome. Like no other event, the Second World War has been dissected and analyzed by historians in every manner conceivable. Often overlooked, however, is the concentrated period of lethal violence in the closing round of the war. Of the millions who perished in the concentration camps, around 30 percent died in the final five months of the war. Most succumbed to the consequences of SS criminal neglect: starvation, exposure, and disease. Others were shot, hanged, or otherwise killed by the SS camp staff and guards.

Rumors had begun circulating in the fall of 1944, the same whispers that caused such a commotion in Manya's camp before her hellish rail journey. Hitler planned to liquidate all prisoners still languishing in the concentration camps. He preferred to destroy the camps and their internees instead of surrendering such indelible evidence of atrocity to the Allies. Hitler confirmed the rumors at a secret cabinet meeting: "I shall conduct this final struggle with all my might and by all available means — I therefore issue this order: empowered to fulfill the final extermination shall be SS national leader [Heinrich] Himmler. . . . Following the course of the war in different areas, or on special order on a pre-determined day, all prisoners in jails, hard labor camps, and concentration camps will be put to death, regardless of whether they are prisoners on remand, convicts, or in preventive arrest, as well as hostages from every country."

Hanging in the balance were the lives of Manya, Lola, and more than 750,000 other prisoners snared by the Nazi death trap over the previous five years who somehow managed to keep breathing until the early days of 1945.

Schutzstaffel Reichsführer Heinrich Himmler, who had

created the concentration camp system, wasted no time implementing the führer's wishes. While his own mental and physical state teetered on the brink, Himmler ordered the complete evacuation of all camps in the east. According to several testimonies, he also issued an ominous warning to the camp commanders: "The führer holds you personally responsible for . . . making sure that not a single prisoner from the concentration camps falls alive into the hands of the enemy."

Among the prisoners still alive were more than 200,000 women, a quarter of whom were held 56 miles north of Berlin in Ravensbrück, the largest and most notorious of Nazi camps for women. Opened in 1939, Ravensbrück adjoined the idyllic Lake Schwedt and was surrounded by pine trees — Nazi leaders believed that the cleansing of German blood should begin close to nature. The German communist Margarete Buber-Neumann, who came to the camp after spending time in a Russian gulag, said of her first impressions of Ravensbrück's perversely beautiful setting, "This is a concentration camp?"

But over the six years of its existence, around 130,000 women passed through its gates, to be beaten, gassed, starved, executed, poisoned, or worked to death. Estimates of the final death toll range from about 30,000 to 90,000; the real figure probably lies somewhere in between, but so few SS documents on the camp survive that no one will ever know for sure. The most serious overcrowding occurred after the evacuation of Auschwitz in January 1945, when an unknown but significant number of Jewish women arrived at Ravensbrück. By then, many of the other camps had been liberated, but Ravensbrück remained fully operational under Nazi control.

During the final weeks of the war, more than 6,000 women were gassed at Ravensbrück. Thousands of others were shot or starved.

From 1939 to 1941, the Nazis had toyed with a variety of techniques to accomplish Hitler's goal of eradicating the Jews. Camp commandants experimented with various killing methods and conferred with each other on their successes and failures, as if they were researchers trying to cure cancer. The capacity to murder hundreds of people per hour at a single camp was no small undertaking; it was a skill that took years to hone and perfect. At first, men, women, and children were simply shot at the edge of vast pits so that their bodies would drop into what became mass graves. In 1941, SS General Erich von dem Bach-Zelewski conveyed to Himmler, by then the second-most powerful man in Germany, his worry that the method may traumatize his men. As Himmler recorded in his diary, "And he said to me, 'Reichsführer, these men are finished for the rest of their lives. What kind of followers are we producing here — either neurotics or brutes?'" At the time, Himmler couldn't have cared less.

The Nazis then experimented with carbon monoxide as a killing agent. But they eventually decided that the most effective and efficient method, developed for Auschwitz, was to use the same pesticide applied to prisoners' clothing to kill lice. The disinfectant, sold under the trade name of Zyklon B, was in plentiful supply and readily available. Once exposed to properly heated air, the crystals exuded a lethal gas. The so-called Final Solution was soon up and running efficiently across the empire.

Filled with self-delusion, and growing increasingly desperate as the Allied armies began advancing into Germany proper, Hitler decided to emulate the defense his armies had encountered in Russia. He issued a number of orders, culminating in the call for total destruction of anything and everything that could be of possible use to the Allies as they advanced. In March 1945, Hitler signed an order to destroy everything of value so that nothing fell into the hands of the Allies. The official command was issued under the heading "Demolitions on Reich Territory" but entered into history as the "Nero Decree," after the Roman emperor who is believed to have deliberately set Rome ablaze in 64 AD.

That decree was a death sentence for hundreds of thousands of Jews and other Europeans still in Nazi custody. In cases where there was no time for mass extermination, prisoners were ordered to take to the road, often in bitter winter weather, so that the camp would be empty when the Allied and Soviet forces turned up. It was one of the war's saddest chapters.

Evacuating prisoners were told nothing about what was happening or where they were going. Many believed they were being taken out to a far-off field to be shot. Instead, they were made to walk for hours in inhumane conditions. Dressed in nothing but rags and wearing wooden shoes, they staggered in the snow and freezing mud. The SS organized them into rows — usually five across — and in large columns, with guards on all sides. The prisoners were forced to keep pace — often at a run. For those already ill, weak, and hungry, it would be impossible. Hours passed. They kept marching. More hours. More marching. Many quickly succumbed to their frailty and could no longer keep up. They fell behind and were summarily shot by SS guards stationed in the rear. At least 250,000 former prisoners — more than one-fourth of them Jews — died on these death marches between January 1945 and May 1945, when Germany finally surrendered. Those who weren't murdered outright died of cold, hunger, and sickness. Today, their graves line the roads surrounding the places where the Nazis built their camps.

One of the largest marches began on January 17, 1945, two months before the Nero Decree, when about 60,000 prisoners from Auschwitz-Birkenau were forced to parade 40 miles under guard, mostly on foot, to Wodzisław Śląski, where they were loaded like cattle onto trucks and trains, and taken to other camps. At least 15,000 prisoners died in the process. Elie Wiesel, winner of the 1986 Nobel Peace Prize, recalled in his 1958 memoir, *Night*, how he and his father were forced to march from Monowitz-Buna, a sub-camp of Auschwitz, to Buchenwald. "Pitch darkness. Every now and then, an explosion in the night. They had orders to fire on any who could not keep up. Their fingers on the triggers, they did not deprive themselves of this pleasure," he wrote. "If one of us had stopped for a second, a sharp shot finished off another filthy son of a bitch. Near me, men were collapsing in the dirty snow. Shots."

It was one of those forced evacuations that led Manya Moszkowicz and her fellow prisoners from the camp in Gleiwitz to the gates of Ravensbrück in January 1945. The camp was even worse than what they had imagined during the 10-day train journey. Emaciated, ghost-like individuals wandered around in a daze. Dead bodies lay everywhere. When they first arrived, they were ushered, terrified, into showers. By now, anyone who had spent any time in the Nazi camps feared the showers. This time, the fear was unwarranted. After a delousing with noxious powder, they retired to the barracks and slept prone for the first time in nearly two weeks.

At Ravensbrück, rising for morning roll call, known as Appell, meant climbing over the corpses of fellow prisoners who had died during the night. The Kapos' shrill whistle marked the start of an interminable daily ritual. Guards calling out the prisoners' numbers waited, often in vain, for faint acknowledgment from the zombie-like figures standing before them. Many of the women fainted from exhaustion as the process ground to a halt and restarted when the numbers didn't add up. Custodians wheeled carts full of corpses, bodies held together only by skin, past the women to the crematorium. Often an arm or a leg would fall off, only to be retrieved and tossed back into the cart like a piece of produce.

"I said to myself, no, I am not going to end up like that. Many times in camp you gave up. You just didn't care how it will end. You just wanted it to end," Manya recalled later. "This cart with the corpses. It doesn't get out of my mind. That's when I said I am not going to end up like this."

A few months later, Manya was moved to Rechlin, a smaller sub-camp of Ravensbrück nearby, where the conditions were not much better. Then, in April 1945, during roll call one morning, a dozen or so women were asked by the Kapo to step forward. By then, the shrieking air raid sirens and roar of Allied bombers were near constant. The women had no inkling what was going on outside the gates, though, and being singled out at camp remained a dangerous proposition. Manya stood with her peers, terrified about what fate might have in store for her that morning.

They were marched to the front gate, where a white truck with red crosses painted on its sides and roof was parked and idling. The tailgate was lowered and the ragtag group of women was told to climb aboard. Weak and emaciated, few had energy enough to raise their feet and struggle inside. One of the Kapos placed a wooden crate to serve as a step and ushered the women toward the bed of the vehicle. Manya was certain she was hallucinating or dreaming.

Inside, the utter disbelief continued. The women were handed packages from the Cooperative for American Remittances to Europe (CARE) bearing labels indicating that they came courtesy of the Canadian government. Inside were powdered milk, cocoa, sardines, and crackers. The ravenous women tore into the packages and gorged on the rations indiscriminately, shoving everything they could into their mouths. Many of them threw up the rations almost as quickly as they consumed them. After years in the camps, their bodies were unaccustomed to anything approaching real nourishment.

The truck bounced west at first, toward Hamburg, over shell-pocked roads and past caravans of war refugees pushing their few belongings in makeshift carts, and then north into occupied Denmark. At Copenhagen, they were loaded onto barges for the crossing to Malmö in Sweden, where the grim caravan (by then the truck had been joined by others bearing the same markings) was met by a reception of waiting clergy, rabbis, and other local dignitaries. Manya and her cohorts, their hair cropped short and matted, their eyes sunken into their skulls, and their skeletal bodies covered in filthy striped dresses tied at the waist with rope, emerged from the trucks to the sounds of a marching band belting out a celebratory ditty.

Manya was in a daze. She felt, she said later, like she was hovering on the edge of the scene while not being part of it, like she was witnessing everything through a sheer curtain. Was their long nightmare finally over? Were they really free?

They were. That night, and in the coming days, the women were given fresh clothes, real soap, and proper showers. They slept in beds with paper sheets. Those who did manage to sleep, anyway. Many of them, including Manya, found themselves staring out the windows of their guesthouses, just to be certain they were not still in the camps and that it was not all just a dream. They were, truly, the lucky ones.

Though she never met him in person, Manya later came to learn the name of the man who orchestrated her escape from Ravensbrück — the dashing Swedish diplomat who dared to breach Hitler's inner circle during the waning days of the Second World War for the sole purpose of saving thousands of strangers the rest of the world had appeared willing to write off.

That man's name was Count Folke Bernadotte.

CHAPTER ONE

Setting the Stage

Manya had grown up a thousand miles away, but she soon fell in love with Sweden. There, she experienced a kindness of spirit she never forgot. On May 8, 1945 — Victory in Europe Day — well-dressed men and women poured out from their homes, waving Swedish flags. Meandering through the clean streets and verdant parks, Manya couldn't get enough of the beauty all around her. Wearing the first clean clothes she'd had in years, she soaked up her surroundings, ready to start a new life.

The country that brought Manya back from the brink of death was the same place where the ancestors of her savior — Folke Bernadotte — had risen to acclaim. But the Sweden of the early 19th century was nothing like the Sweden of the 1940s. To better understand Folke Bernadotte's incredible act of humanity, it's helpful to see where he came from.

Far from the egalitarian paradise of tidy stoops, good government, and flush Nordic cheeks that it was to become, the Stockholm of the early 1800s was little more than a bit player on the European stage — a stagnant city surrounded by slums, with a dwindling population, rampant alcoholism, abysmal public health, and widespread unemployment. Upper-class visitors from other European countries described Sweden as a whole as a poor and backwater place made up mostly of nondescript towns and villages.

All cities cycle through periods of boom and bust, but Stockholm's rise and fall was particularly precipitous. Founded in the 13th century, it grew to be a major European power in the 17th century when it forcefully took control of huge swaths of the Baltic region upon which Europe was reliant for such staples as grain, iron ore, timber, copper, and furs. The population grew exponentially during this period, and by the turn of the 17th century, Stockholm had become the center of a vast Swedish empire. Swedes called this period Stormaktstiden, or the Era of Great Power. The empire extended well into Poland and Russia, as well as a colony on the Delaware River in North America around what is now Philadelphia.

The Plague put an end to that in short order, wiping out a third of the population in 1710. The shell of a country that remained was decimated by the Great Northern War, a series of battles with its Scandinavian neighbors. Routed by the Russians in 1709, the brilliant but irascible Swedish king, Karl XII, and his troops fled south into the Ottoman Empire, where they remained, trapped in exile, for five years. He returned home too late to salvage his empire, and the spoils were divided among the allied powers of Russia, Saxony-Poland, and Denmark-Norway. The 1750s marked the beginning of a century of decline for Sweden.

By the early 1800s, much of Stockholm's population of about 70,000 was crowded around the Royal Palace in what is now known as the Old Town, an island in the main waterway connecting the freshwater Lake Mälaren with the Baltic Sea. Today, it is a charming labyrinth of cobbled streets and winding alleyways lined with cafes, restaurants, artists' studios, and purveyors of tourist trinkets. Then, it was largely a fetid slum, its unpaved streets dotted with taverns full of drunk patrons coughing themselves to death from tuberculosis and alleys where prostitutes with bared breasts plied their bodies from windows and doorways. Other women lived in crowded, often windowless rooms with floors of stamped dirt. There, they sat at spinning wheels all day after sending their preteen children out to collect human excrement door-to-door in cans that they would deliver across the water of Mälaren to the saltpeter refinery, where gunpowder was made.

Even for men, employment was catch-as-catch-can. Soldiers in the royal barracks often moonlighted as cobblers or other tradesmen to supplement their meager salaries, and those lucky enough to find work during the relatively abundant summer months were often jobless and destitute again when winter's dark days returned. Consumption, fevers, stroke, and edema contributed to one of the highest mortality rates in Europe. Between 1750 and 1850, there were only four years in which Stockholm saw more births than deaths. Marriage rates plunged, and out-of-wedlock births — or "bastardy," in the charming parlance of later economists — skyrocketed.

Death was always just around the corner. Graveyards were said to be so overloaded that skulls and bones poked out from beneath mounds of fresh dirt. If malnourishment (the average Stockholm resident subsisted largely on a diet of bread, potatoes, and oats) or drink (brännvin, a brandy made from potatoes or grain, was a fixture of nearly every meal, even for children) didn't do one in, then the extras that made their way into the diet would have for certain. One female silver polisher complained in 1800 that a loaf of bread she had purchased from a local bakery had a whole rat at its core, "from which an evil taste arose." A shoemaker arriving in Stockholm around this time concluded that "the Stockholm life had produced such feelings of unpleasantness and cheerlessness that I decided to travel to another country, no matter which one." He moved to St. Petersburg before eventually settling in Paris.

All this set the stage for the founding of the House of Bernadotte, a royal dynasty that continues to this day.

By the first decade of the 19th century, much of Europe was mired in war and revolution. Sweden's King Karl XIII's two children had died in infancy, and his adopted son and successor, Prince Karl August, also passed away suddenly in 1810. The country was in turmoil with no heir to lead it. This drove Sweden's ruling parliament, the Riksdag, to look outside the country for a fresh face to fortify the teetering monarchy. They found it in the countenance of Jean-Baptiste Jules Bernadotte, one of Napoleon's top generals and one of Folke Bernadotte's most distinguished and dashing ancestors. Jean-Baptiste's spectacular rise in the ranks may partly be due to his marriage to Désirée Clary, Napoleon's first love. Despite the famously fickle French leader's marriage in 1798 to the widow Joséphine de Beauharnais, Napoleon continued to care about and look after Clary's well-being for the rest of his life. Jean-Baptiste's military prowess also caught the eye of Napoleon, who eventually made him a Marshal of France, one of the highest honors of the era.

Why the Swedes would put an ambitious middle-aged French marshal, the son of a lawyer, in line for the throne had much to do with the existing royal family's own desperation. They had lost Finland, an integral part of Sweden for seven centuries, to Russia in 1807. After such a humiliating defeat, a bold action was called for. The hope was that Jean-Baptiste, a talented soldier who had shown much prowess on the battlefield, would help them take back Finland as well as steady the wobbling monarchy itself. And so Bernadotte came to Sweden and assumed the title of Crown Prince under the name Karl Johan (Karl, after the king who had been on the throne, and Johan as the Swedish version of Jean). Very soon, though, he made it clear to the ruling nobles that he had no intention of trying to get Finland back. In his opinion, it would be military suicide. Instead, he set his sights on a prize he was certain he could win — Norway. Still a determined and courageous commander, Karl Johan put enormous military pressure on Denmark (an ally of France and Napoleon that ruled over Norway at the time) and succeeded in preventing the territory from gaining its independence and instead forced it to join in a union with Sweden through the Treaty of Kiel in 1814. The campaign to prevent Norway's secession was to be the last war Sweden ever fought.

Karl Johan and Désirée had only one son, Oscar I, who inherited the throne after the death of his father in

1844. But a protracted period of bad health cast a pall, and Oscar's reign lasted a mere 15 years, until he died in 1859. His eldest son, who succeeded him as Karl XV, was handsome and charming, the very embodiment of a king. In time, though, his power was greatly diminished as the Riksdag assumed more authority. Karl left one child, Louisa Josephina Eugenia, by his marriage to Louisa — the daughter of Prince Frederik of the Netherlands — and was succeeded by his brother, Oscar II, in 1872.

Oscar II, Folke Bernadotte's grandfather, reigned over a revival in Sweden referred to as the "Great Transformation." The backward agricultural nation of the previous century was evolving into a modern industrial economy that laid the groundwork for the welfare state that would follow in the 20th century. The country's abundant natural resources had much to do with the economic growth of the era. There were timber booms in both the 1850s and 1870s, and when the forests were exhausted, the Swedes figured out a way to turn wood pulp into paper and revolutionized the global publishing industry. Iron ore exports to Europe ratcheted up, as did local steel production. Ericson started making telephones in 1876, and by the 1890s Stockholm was one of the world's great telecommunications capitals. Gas works, sewage, and water mains were introduced to the city, and streets were paved. Stockholm cleaned up nicely and was like a whole new city.

Oscar II ruled with the best intentions as he navigated the deteriorating relations between Norway and Sweden, which share a 1,000-mile border. But under his rule, the two sides' interests diverged beyond the point of reconciliation. Discontent simmered and eventually boiled over, with Norway believing that Sweden treated it as a junior partner; calls for autonomy grew louder. In the spring of 1905, the Norwegian government voted for independence. In a public referendum, over 99 percent of Norwegian voters favored dissolution, and Sweden had little choice but to negotiate a formal end to the union. On October 26, 1905, Oscar II officially renounced his claim to the Norwegian throne and Sweden finally recognized Norway as an independent constitutional monarchy.

When not delicately handling the Norwegians, Oscar II concentrated his efforts on artistic ventures, the remnants of which are still enjoyed today. He established the world's first open-air museum, near his summer residence in Kristiania (now Oslo) in 1881, and he commissioned a new opera house for the Royal Swedish Opera in the 1890s. He also was a prolific author, writing the memoirs of King Karl XII along with his own. He was so self-assured when it came to the arts that he once told celebrated Norwegian playwright Henrik Ibsen at a dinner held in Ibsen's honor that his famous *Ghosts* was "not a good play" and should never have been written. After a moment of stunned silence, Ibsen replied that writing it was preordained: "Your Majesty, I *had* to write *Ghosts*." In 1907, as he lay dying, Oscar II asked that the theaters not be closed in the event of his death, as was tradition. The country respected his wishes.

Oscar II passed away in Stockholm, after which the eldest of Oscar's four sons, and Folke's uncle, became King Gustaf V. Like his father, Gustaf V proved to be a capable and enlightened leader, and is considered one of the more outstanding monarchs in a thousand years of more or less sustained royal Swedish distinction. In a break with tradition going back nearly 700 years, Gustaf V cancelled the grand ceremonies associated with a formal coronation. He also opted against wearing a crown, a custom that continues to this day. Gustaf V championed a long list of social reforms, among them an eight-hour workday, employer-provided accident insurance, and government subsidized low-income housing. Most notably, he confirmed the deep-seated change in Swedish society by helping enact universal and equal suffrage, including for women, in 1919. He was the type of monarch who enjoyed strolling the streets, stopping to talk with surprised passersby along the way, a practice that earned him the reputation of being "the people's royalty." In 1881, he married Victoria of Baden.

Gustaf V was a devoted player and a grand patron of tennis, a game he picked up in 1878 during a trip to England, years before he became king; after returning to Sweden, he founded the country's first tennis club. When given the option, he'd always take chasing balls on a casual court over listening to opera in a fancy theater. He played tennis privately and competitively — usually under the name "Mr. G" or another pseudonym — well into his 90s.

From his uncle, Folke Bernadotte inherited a burning sense of fair play and honor. From his parents, the overarching lesson must surely have been that in the face of true love, everything else must be cast aside. Indeed, the story of Folke's parents' courtship can only be described as a fairy tale, even though it meant that Folke would never ascend to the throne in Stockholm.

Born on November 15, 1859, Folke's father, Prince Oscar Carl August, was the second son of the future King Oscar II and Queen Sophia of Sweden and Norway. Like his father, Prince Oscar was a dutiful servant and joined the navy at an early age. But his future took a left turn after he met the woman who would become Folke's mother, Ebba Munck, a dazzling young lady-in-waiting to the Crown Princess Victoria.

Oscar's stated desire to marry Munck set off an immediate scandal. The Swedish constitution prohibited princes of the royal house from marrying non-royals, even if they were from a noble family. Oscar begged to be allowed to renounce his birthright. But his stubborn father wouldn't hear of it. Although the Munck family was definitely a respectable one — Ebba was the daughter of the well-regarded Colonel Carl Jacob Munck and Baroness Henrica Cederstrom — the king opposed what he considered a "misalliance."

In an attempt to change his mind, Oscar's parents shipped him off on a two-year journey around the globe, a trip that would afford him plenty of time to contemplate his future. He was discharged from royal service, and Ebba was dismissed as a lady-in-waiting. (Victoria also did not approve of the relationship.) But when he returned, Oscar assured his family that he and Ebba were still determined to marry. Oscar's father remained dead set against the match but, much to his chagrin, an unlikely ally came to Oscar's rescue. That ally was Oscar's mother, Sophia, who had always been a level-headed woman and a reliable advisor to family and friends.

And she was headstrong. Sophia had never been afraid to go up against her sons or her husband, and she put enormous pressure on Oscar II to sanction their second son's marriage to the woman he loved. Oscar held his ground — but so did Sophia, who told him, "It is Oscar's duty to be true to himself and to his life." Both sides dug in. Since the reigning house of Sweden and Norway was one of the newest of the royal houses of Europe, Oscar II believed it to be more necessary than ever that its scions should intermarry so that bloodlines could be secured.

But in a twist of fate, the queen suddenly fell quite ill, suffering from mysterious knife-like stabbing pains in her stomach that sidelined her for weeks. Her only chance for survival, according to the doctors, was a risky surgical procedure called an ovariotomy that was at the very least agonizingly uncomfortable and at the worst life-threatening. Before the operation, she summoned the king to her bedside, where she gave him an ultimatum: "If I undergo this operation and recover, will you allow Oscar and Ebba to have their way?" The king adored his wife and would have done anything to reassure her, and so of course he caved. The operation was successful, and after it was clear the queen would recover, the king made good on his promise to allow the marriage, but only after Oscar's three brothers signed a document vowing to never enter into a similar morganatic relationship.

The wedding of Folke's parents took place on March 15, 1888, in the seaside town of Bournemouth, England. By marrying a commoner, Prince Oscar was automatically stripped of his right of succession to the Swedish and Norwegian thrones. He was, however, allowed to keep his title of prince, to which he added the surname Bernadotte. He became Prince Oscar Bernadotte after renouncing his Norwegian citizenship, and his wife became Princess Ebba Bernadotte. Their children were referred to simply as Mr. and Miss until Oscar's descendants in the agnatic line were granted the title of Count(ess) of Wisborg. While royal family members would never consider Ebba a fit match for Oscar, the public saw it differently, and they showered the couple with support and sympathy. To them, Ebba represented something of a bridge between commoners and royals — "The Munck Bridge" — bringing the king and queen closer to their subjects. When the couple left Stockholm for their wedding in England, thousands of well-wishers turned out to bid them farewell.

Such was the household into which Folke Bernadotte was born on January 2, 1895. Because of Prince Oscar's naval duties, the family first lived in Karlskrona, a naval city spread over 30 islands, but later settled into a house on Östermalmsgatan 56 in Stockholm's business district. The medium-sized dwelling was modest and not even remotely regal. The only real decorations were pieces of religious art such as a painting of the Virgin Mary holding baby Jesus. But there was a pleasant porch that granted views of the busy street beyond the small garden plot out front. For their entire married life, Oscar and Ebba lived frugally, deriving their greatest satisfaction not from the trappings of material wealth, but from helping the underprivileged. Ebba was deeply religious and influenced Oscar in this regard, so much so that he eventually became a dedicated lay preacher. Like most Swedes, they were active Lutherans. Not only were they both involved in the church, but they also dedicated any free time and energy to the YMCA, the Salvation Army, and similar organizations.

Coddled as the youngest of five children and the second long-limbed and broad-shouldered son, Folke later recalled his childhood with warm affection. But his upbringing was also strict, he noted, and actions in the household were never without consequences. Oscar was a loving but stern father who imposed on his children an inflexible daily diet of prayer, learning, and good works on behalf of those less fortunate.

Folke later wrote that "My father often said a child should learn to obey before it reached two years of age. My parents very much insisted on honesty, obedience and punctuality. Already when we were small our thoughts were directed towards trying to help others. My father and his brother had themselves been brought up in the same atmosphere and my parents sought to continue the traditions which my grandmother had founded." Growing up, Folke said he never heard his parents exchange so much as an angry word. "Their relationship was characterized by an unselfish appreciation of each other's wishes," he said.

Folke's childhood was secure and comfortable, and punctuated by the many traditional Nordic rituals that make the long, dreary winters a bit more bearable. In December, the sun never rises before 8 a.m., and by 4 p.m. it's already setting. Christmas celebrations are elaborate by design as they served to brighten the otherwise dismal season. The festivities start with St. Lucia Day, a Christian feast day held every December 13 that became popular in the 1800s and pays tribute to St. Lucia, the fourth-century Italian woman said to have been one of the first Christian martyrs. Families still mark the occasion by dressing their eldest daughters in long white gowns with red ribbons tied around the waist. Tradition has it that Lucia is to wear "light in her hair," which in practice means a crown of fresh greens and lit candles (today they are electric). The event has come to symbolize the idea of light overcoming darkness and the promise of returning sunshine. The processions held across the country on St. Lucia Day were, and still are, illuminated by thousands of candles.

The Swedes love Christmas so much that the celebrations start in earnest the day before, on Christmas Eve, when presents are exchanged and the smorgasbord known as the julbord is piled high with meatballs, pickled herring, potato gratin, rice porridge, and other holiday foods. Plenty of time is set aside for family and friends, and for helping the poor. The Bernadottes were no different, and on Christmas Eve, the entire clan gathered in Stockholm's baroque Royal Palace, a grand structure with more than 600 rooms divided among seven floors, to celebrate. The day before that, "Little Christmas Eve" on December 23, the family would share ham and other foods, as well as little gifts, with their servants and the needy. Often, the Bernadottes hosted a holiday party for members of their staff, at which Swedish folk dancing was among the lively entertainment.

The only Swedish holiday to rival Christmas time in festive spirit and traditions is Midsummer's Night, which celebrates the longest day of the year every June. People kick off the day by picking flowers and crafting wreaths and placing them on a maypole raised in an open spot. Quaint ring dances ensue, followed by more riotous gatherings in the evening, lubricated by beer and vodka, and topped off with herring. The magic of midsummer often includes a celebration of nature and divination of the future, especially the identity of one's future spouse. As darkness descended, the families of the four princes, Oscar, Karl, Eugene, and their eldest brother, King Gustaf, and their children gathered to revel in the festivities like any other Swedish family.

The holidays marked the few times of year when the Bernadotte children were allowed and even encouraged to be frivolous and socialize. The rest of the time, real playmates were often in short supply, as the strict Bernadotte home was hardly a congenial setting for silly kids that just wanted to have fun. If Folke and his siblings did play a game, it was "of the typical guessing variety," and not terribly exciting. In general, friends rather dreaded getting an invite to the home. The most spirited of the Bernadotte children was Folke's second sister, Sophia, and even she never found her way into a public ballroom until 1932, when she was 40 and visiting Monte Carlo. Maria, the oldest sister, was a serious sort. She eventually worked as a nurse and never married. The other sister, Elsa, married the secretary of the Young Men's Christian Association, Hugo Cedergren. Folke's brother, Carl, married a baroness in 1915, but they divorced 20 years later.

Folke may have had more in common with his cousins, who were not overly intellectual. Together they skied, skated, and rode horses. Folke could be a curious boy, and he loved being outdoors, but he lacked drive and focus and exhibited few signs of being a motivated learner. Also undercutting his scholarly prospects was his dyslexia, a condition that was not given official recognition until 1994 and was known at the time as "word-blindness." The learning disability apparently plagued many in the Bernadotte family and made reading a struggle. Not surprisingly, this provoked little appetite for literature in the young Folke. His reading habits rarely evolved beyond a penchant for sneak-reading comic books when he was growing up, with the exception, of course, of the Bible, which was part of the family's daily life along with morning and evening prayers, and grace before every meal.

The family almost never failed to attend church — twice — on Sundays, and the siblings rarely left the house on Saturday evenings. Folke's three sisters had inherited a penchant for sewing from their mother and so, rather than going out, they spent that time teaching poor people how to stitch their own clothes. So as not to make the sisters jealous, Folke and his elder brother Carl were ordered to stay home as well. The boys took the routine in stride — they had no choice — even as their contemporaries were out enjoying Stockholm's social scene. Folke wrote, "I will freely admit that I didn't look forward to those sewing evenings with any enthusiasm. I would far rather have been together with my classmates from Nya Elementar who might have offered something more attractive to a young man full of the joy of living."

Nya Elementar was a day school around the corner from their home, attended by both Folke and his brother. Their classmates represented a broad cross-section of mostly upper-middle-class Swedish society — the sons of actors, diplomats, and businessmen. Folke's royal background engendered a sense of separation, but his athletic prowess, especially at horseback riding, helped him fit in with a small circle of friends. He also wasn't above getting his hands dirty, and he spent his free time hunting for bugs in the garden around his home. In many ways, he was a typical boy, one who so far had manifested no signs of inherent leadership potential. If he'd only been a bit more studious, or not had dyslexia, he might have gone on to be quite the academic after having enjoyed a good education at such respectable schools. But that was not the case. During those early years, Folke did not appear to be cut out for any of the career options normally available to royalty.

But he had some skills that would prove valuable later in life. In 1904, at the age of nine, Folke traveled abroad for the first time, to England with his parents. That trip had a big impact on him: English became one of his best school subjects and his second tongue. Indeed, he had much more of a knack for foreign languages — he became fluent in French and German as well — than he ever had for math or writing. It's no surprise that his other best subject was religion, which had been stamped upon him throughout childhood. In 1909, he was confirmed at the Messiah Chapel in Stockholm, at the age of 14. During the weekends, he was privy to his sisters' frequent gatherings of missionaries, which aroused in him a curiosity about foreign affairs. But international welfare work held no real appeal for him at this early stage. And since there was no radio and he read little beyond the Bible, Folke's lack of interest in the world outside Sweden was palpable.

One event, possibly apocryphal, foreshadowed events to come. In Folke's fourth-grade class at Nya, the teacher asked the pupils what they hoped to be when they grew up.

One answered after another, while young Folke sat back silently, apparently trying to formulate a proper response in his head, as if this were the most serious question he'd ever been asked. After careful deliberation, he replied, "I shall be a papa." Sentimental Swedes now see a prophetic meaning behind that simple statement: that he would not only be a father in the conventional sense of the word, but also a father figure — a protector — for many thousands of vulnerable human beings. But, of course, he was no prophesier. He was just another ordinary Swedish youth, with no way of knowing what an extraordinary life lay before him.

CHAPTER TWO

A Brush with Death

The trickle of changes that came to Sweden throughout the 19th century turned into a torrent with the turn of the century, and the awkward young boy from Nya Elementar was swept along with it at a dizzying pace. No facet of society was immune to the rapid innovation. The agricultural revolution introduced large-scale and technically advanced methods of cultivating the land. Fed by the country's enormous hydroelectric potential, a flourishing electrical industry emerged. Even the hidebound military found itself struggling to keep up with the changes, as young Folke — prepped nearly from birth for a career in the armed forces — was soon to discover.

Perspectives of space and time were shifting. In 1898, a Polish and French-naturalized chemist called Marie Curie coined the term "radioactivity." A German-born physicist named Albert Einstein wrote about the theory of relativity in 1905. An American inventor, Thomas Edison, produced the first talking movies by combining his phonograph with a kinetoscope, a peephole-equipped box that was the preferred method of watching moving pictures at the time. Those same phonographs became a staple in most households, both rich and poor. Eastman Kodak introduced the Brownie box camera in 1900, which sold for $1 and opened the previously rarefied world of photography to ordinary folks. General Electric built the first electric toaster for the home in 1909, changing the way people ate breakfast, and the compact vacuum cleaner roared to life on filthy rugs everywhere.

Sweden latched onto the talking pictures phenomenon slowly, reluctantly even, but made up for lost time later and became inextricably entwined with the technology in the world's popular imagination. Early silent movies were such crowd-pleasers that promoters were hesitant to shift to the new sound-infused format for fear of cutting into their lucrative export earnings. Only the introduction of radio, or AB Radiotjänst, as Swedish Radio was originally called, on New Year's Day in 1925, when Folke was 30 years old, forced them to reconsider. Among the iconic names that came to dominate cinema were Ingmar Bergman, born in 1918 in Stockholm, who went on to become one of the most accomplished and influential filmmakers of all time, and actress Ingrid Bergman, who launched her career in Sweden in the 1930s and went on to become one of Hollywood's greatest leading actresses, winning three Academy Awards.

By the early 1900s, the Swedish manufacturing sector — powered initially by steam but later by electricity and the internal combustion engine as well — churned out iron, steel, timber, and other goods for export at accelerated rates. At that time, Britain and a few other countries were already well underway in the industrial development process. Although Sweden was, industrially speaking, something of a slow starter, the country stepped into the global arena at just the right moment. The economic development in Europe increased international demand and created a profitable market for Sweden's raw materials, particularly lumber. Giving Sweden a big advantage was the country's abundance of natural resources, such as iron ore, timber, and hydroelectric power — the plethora of rivers and waterfalls in the north of the country made electricity a relatively cheap commodity. This, in turn, lowered costs and further raised the demand for Swedish products on the international market. Due to an overall increase in incomes, the domestic market for products also picked up.

The industrialization of the late 19th and early 20th centuries was in lockstep with the growth of a labor movement that pushed for concessions from employers and cemented the country's reputation as a haven for generous social policies. The first unions emerged in the 1880s among the new urban working classes, but it wasn't until the 1920s and 1930s that they began seriously flexing their muscles, ushering in such benefits as paid vacations, subsidized childcare, and maternity pay aimed at replacing about 80 percent of a woman's net earnings. Even today, more than 70 percent of the working population belongs to a union.

Beyond the workplace, an increasingly enlightened urban middle class moved the country to the forefront on all sorts of social issues. Universal suffrage was introduced for men in 1909 and for women in 1919. During the 1920s and 1930s, the first baby steps were taken toward the development of a generous welfare state. The concept of the country as a

"People's Home" — a place with room for everyone — caught on and began to exemplify the ideal Swedish way of life. In 1909, Sweden became the first country in Europe to legalize protection of the landscape with the establishment of a national parks system, and to this day all lands and lakes are open to the public under Sweden's right to public access, known as allemansrätt, or "the everyman's right." The principle, enshrined in the nation's constitution, means that skiers, hikers, and cyclists are free to roam almost anywhere they like, with minor exceptions such as private gardens or the immediate vicinity of someone's home.

Though it remained on the sidelines of military conflict through much of the 19th century, Sweden came to play an inadvertently outsized role in the development of the modern military machine during the early 20th. Alfred Nobel — the man behind the celebrated annual prizes for peace, medicine, literature, and other endeavors of the human spirit — invented both dynamite and a reliable method of setting it off, with a blasting cap, in his laboratory near Stockholm in the 1860s. His desire was to design a dependable explosive for the construction and mining industries, but the solution he devised also revolutionized warfare. When Nobel died in 1896, he was said to be so distraught by his reputation as a man of death that he left much of his vast fortune to the prizes that bear his name and celebrate less bellicose improvements to humanity's repertoire.

Nobel's dynamite, and the rockets and cannons that followed, changed the way wars are waged, putting an end to centuries of military traditions. Rolling artillery like tanks, for example, brought down the curtain on the cavalry units to which the Swedish royal family had turned for generations as the favored form of serving their country. In 1915, when Folke was 20 and beginning his obligatory military service, the first prototype tank, nicknamed Little Willie, rolled off an assembly line in England. Initially able to crawl over a rugged landscape at only two miles per hour, Little Willie was far from an overnight success. But in the following years, the design was tweaked so that the behemoths — weighing as much as 18 tons — could more easily navigate tough terrain, and they eventually transformed the battlefield. The armored vehicle made its active debut in 1916 at the First Battle of the Somme, near Courcelette, France, at first garnering only mixed reviews because the tanks had a bad habit of breaking down. Consistently reliable or not, the vehicles proved to be a massive morale boost for the British during the First World War. German troops were terrified of them.

Folke Bernadotte came from a long line of distinguished military men. Not only was he the nephew of King Gustaf V, the last Swedish monarch to serve as commander-in-chief of the military — a duty the uncle took seriously and one he diligently performed until 1939 — but, of course, he also bore the name of one of Napoleon's most celebrated marshals. There was never any question that Folke would join the military, and a career in the cavalry was likely mapped out for him as soon as he could walk. All members of the royal family were expected to lead by example, and to do their part for national security.

But they couldn't have used their status to skirt their duties even if they'd wanted to. Sweden first introduced universal conscription in 1901, and not even royals were exempt from obligatory service. Every able-bodied Swedish man was expected to undergo military instruction at the age of 18. Each year, new recruits were drafted for military training. When one set of recruits finished training, a new set took its place. Those who passed their initial tests and were approved for service were assigned to a division of the army (cavalry, infantry, artillery), the navy, or the air force. Before tank and trench warfare took hold, there were multiple branches of cavalry. The hussars carried sabers and rifles and typically fought from the horse, while lancers wielded long javelin-like spears and charged at lines of infantry. The dragoons were mounted infantry men who usually dismounted their horses in the thick of battle. Military training generally consisted of a basic education period of about 360 days — although this varied depending on the posting — followed by three compulsory military refresher courses of 30 days each. The draftees spent their days practicing such skills as riflery and the care of arms and the ability to parade around in front of the officers in perfect lockstep. They learned to handle weapons as naturally as they did a knife and fork.

So, after finishing up at Nya, Folke entered the Military Academy Karlberg, the Swedish West Point, at the age of 18. The Karlberg Palace, built in 1630 with a main building stretching more than 720 feet, has hosted a military academy since 1792, making it the oldest such institution in the world still operating in its original location. The gleaming white structure sits perched on a lake in Solna, adjacent to a former royal summer residence and northwest of central Stockholm. The serene setting was ideal for someone like Folke, who so enjoyed the outdoors. Not only was the palace spectacular, but Solna was (and remains) one of Sweden's lovelier municipalities, with a finger-like saltwater lake, Brunnsviken, dominating the east side and surrounded by idyllic meadows. On the lake's western shore was Hagaparken, one of Europe's best-preserved English landscape parks. Founded by Folke's ancestor, King Gustaf III, near the end of the 18th century, it offers winding footpaths, scenic views, and assorted pavilions such as the Temple of Echo, built in 1790 as a picturesque outdoor dining room for royalty. Since 1922, Hagaparken has been home to the Royal Cemetery, where most members of the royal Bernadotte family have been laid to rest. Also buried there are Alfred Nobel and Ingrid Bergman, as well as many other noteworthy figures. This vast green area is still one of Stockholm's most popular places to gather.

His parents instilled in Folke the value of a strong character and a devout faith in God, but it was the military that matured him. Time in the service taught him new skills and polished the ones he already had — skills that could be applied to everyday life. He learned to pack his belongings and be ready to move at a moment's notice. He learned to brave the wild in even the harshest of conditions. He learned how to give orders, take orders, and manage others with authority. He learned how to evaluate and respond decisively to a threat. Because he was from such a strict household, self-discipline came easy, and he exhibited signs of being a competent leader early on in his military life. On parade, he stood up straight and tall and marched proudly in his uniform. No matter what the regiment, all men wore the same clothes: a blue coat with yellow cuffs and stockings — Sweden's national colors. Off parade, though,

Folke sometimes found it a bit harder to find his footing. As a royal, he couldn't easily foster brotherhood across class boundaries.

But he did manage to squeeze in some fun. Five days a week, the military men worked hard, and on weekends they returned to their parents' homes. Only on weekday evenings did they enjoy a few hours out on their own. Folke was more than adept at following the weekend routine at home, but his rigid upbringing and conservative views reined him in during the week. For the most part, he shied away from heavy drinking and wild carousing, but he was an occasional patron of the Blanche Black Cat Bar, a somewhat decadent haunt with an anything goes atmosphere that was popular among those studying at Karlberg. The famous restaurant at the center of Stockholm was known for hiring the prettiest waitresses — a nearly irresistible draw for young aristocrats that often had little contact with females beyond cousins and sisters. Being something of a novice when it came to mingling with the opposite sex, Folke no doubt found himself unwillingly exposed to the most titillating atmosphere he'd ever experienced. With the men's venerable blue uniforms — not to mention their often-famous surnames — it wasn't unusual for romantic attachments to spring up. Folke put in a few appearances at Blanche parties, but never fully embraced the party culture. When it came to that final, fatal "last call" drink — or the question of whether or not to take a girl home — he invariably begged off, a response indicative of a more primal fear: doing something that would sully his family's fine reputation.

On December 20, 1915, 20-year-old Folke was given the military ranking of Ensign more or less automatically, as the king's nephew, in the 90 percent blue-blooded Royal Life Guard Dragoons, having ranked a respectable 10th in his year's class at the military school. As a dragoon, or an elite member of the cavalry, Folke was able to study horsemanship at the Strömsholm Riding School in 1916. Strömsholm was also a good fit for the lanky and outdoorsy Folke. Like the military school of Karlberg, the aristocratic Strömsholm is located in picturesque surroundings, next to the yellow Baroque-style Strömsholm Castle in the county of Västmanland. It was the perfect place for a cavalry school, as the country for miles around was level and covered in a strong turf. By the time Folke arrived at Strömsholm, it had been the national education center of equestrian sport for centuries.

Folke had always loved horses, and for the rest of his life, riding remained one of his favorite hobbies, one he indulged in as much as his health and work would allow. He showed marked ability as a horseman and won an array of prizes; in his prime, he was one of the finest of Sweden's many superb horsemen. And so it was the horses in large part that made life in the military more palatable for Folke. As a dragoon, he and the other cavalry members were trained to fight while mounted on horseback, giving them a mobility and height advantage that would intimidate foot soldiers. In true medieval feudal style, officers and enlisted men alike provided their own horses, which helped each man feel as though he had a personal stake in the regiment.

With roots that go back as far as 1523, the Dragoons are one of the world's oldest military units and the only mounted unit still retained by the Swedish Army. The name is derived from a type of firearm, called a "dragon," a hand-held version of a blunderbuss, carried by dragoons of the French Army. In Sweden, King Gustav II Adolf introduced dragoons into the Swedish Army, providing them with a sabre, an axe, and later a matchlock musket — which had the advantage of a faster rate of fire. All of this made the country's cavalry a much-feared force. As machine guns and tanks became the norm, though, the cavalry started to disappear from the battlefields, and the First World War was the last war to see horsemen in action. Today, horses are used in the Swedish Army only for ceremonial purposes, most often when the dragoons take part in the changing of the guards at the Royal Palace in Stockholm.

The dragoons were just about the last bastion of Swedish medievalism on the eve of the socialist age. Breeding, education, and character all came into play when seeking to obtain a commission in this, the most exclusive unit of the Swedish Army. The rank and file were equally select in their own way. The regiments were a holdover from medieval times, when the feudal Swedish barons — not unlike their prototypes in other lands — raised their quota of men for the defense of the realm. Since the cream of the Swedish gentry officered the Life Guard Dragoons, the most talented of yeomen were to serve in this regiment. The Life Guard Dragoons were akin to an exclusive university fraternity, with all the advantages of tremendous loyalty but with the disadvantage of upper-crust snobbishness. They lived in a tiny closed-off cocoon in which anybody on the outside was considered more or less inconsequential. If not for the love of the horses, the Life Guard Dragoons' insular world might have suffocated and displeased a young man like Folke, a do-gooder who was forever bothered by any gulf between the rich and the poor.

Later in life, after Folke had seen more of the world, he would hardly have tolerated this type of pretension, even as he appreciated the regiment's camaraderie and devotion. Service in the Life Guard Dragoons was a hallmark of prestige, patriotism, and reliability, and it garnered a lot of respect. The motto of the dragoons was "They can do what it seems they cannot." That and the motto of Folke's Regiment, "Serve Only Honor," inspired his conduct for the rest of his life. Because he was excluded from the line to the throne as a result of his mother's commoner status, "the service, horses and pleasures captured my entire interest," he wrote years later. "I do not believe that I was aware of any emptiness in my life. My personal motto was to live life with a smile."

Folke was dead set on a military career and had every intention of becoming a professional soldier — his ultimate goal was to become a senior cavalry commander and not just one of those men who joined the regiment as a stepping stone to another career. And there was a lot that might have made Folke a standout soldier. Not only was he a solid leader, but his gift at languages (he eventually became fluent in six) gave him a leg up. But although Folke's star rose quickly — he became a lieutenant in 1918 and subsequently achieved the rank of major — it was apparent that he would not be able to advance any further. The reason? His stubbornly poor health.

Never the most robust of children, Folke suffered sporadic bouts of stomach pain throughout his youth. At first, he dismissed these as a minor annoyance, but they ballooned into a full-blown health crisis in 1916 when he was 21. Folke was on a grueling nighttime cavalry patrol when suddenly he slumped off his horse, unconscious, and tumbled to the ground. One of his comrades examined him by lantern light and was sickened to find his clothes moist not with sweat, but with blood. He was sure Folke was dying. Folke roused himself and tried to stand, but he stumbled again and fell to his knees, too weak to take even a single step. He was rushed to the hospital. Although he returned to normal within a few weeks, the episode would be the beginning of a lifelong, and at times incapacitating, web of health issues surrounding stomach ulcers and the rectal bleeding often associated with it.

Complications arising from stomach ulcers are fairly uncommon, but they can be life-threatening. The primary symptoms of bloating and heartburn are only the tip of the iceberg. Pain from a stomach ulcer can travel, radiating between your back, your belly button, and your breastbone, and a bleeding ulcer can lead to anemia, fatigue, and fainting. It can also cause you to vomit bright red blood, which may be another reason Folke's clothes were wet with it. From then on, Folke required massive injections of vitamin C — a major antioxidant that protects the lining of the stomach — as well as intermittent stints in the hospital. Though he almost never complained or even talked about his condition, he had, at 21, come face-to-face with his own mortality. "He had a feeling that his hemorrhages eventually might lead to his death because his maternal grandfather succumbed to a series of them," a family member later recalled.

Even though his recurring condition occasionally forced him to spend weeks confined to a hospital bed, only a few of his closest friends and family members were even aware of it. Ever the optimist, Folke reacted to his confinement with intense introspection. "Life in a hospital is certainly somewhat depressing," he wrote. "But I would nevertheless not have that experience undone. When one doesn't know how the future will turn out, and when one realizes that the distance between life and death is short, at that moment the importance of all difficulties disappears, although they normally bulk so large. . . . I am glad that I had that experience in the hospital. It was of great use to me." He quickly came to terms with his physical disability, learning to live with it just as he had his dyslexia. If anything, it gave him even greater empathy for others, softening even more any barriers he may have felt between himself and the socially disadvantaged. Being hospitalized for long stretches also honed a mental toughness that made him a stronger and more self-assured man.

On the heels of his health scare came another close brush with death. In the winter of 1918, Folke, by this time a lieutenant in the cavalry, was riding on the frozen Deer Park Bridge Creek in the outskirts of Stockholm when the ice suddenly gave way under his horse's weight. The animal was flailing frantically and, although horses can swim, the freezing water quickly took a toll, exhausting it, and before long, his horse was sucked down below the surface. Rather than think of his own well-being, the 23-year-old cavalry officer sprang into action, trying everything he could to get the horse out, even plunging into the frigid black hole himself in an attempt to rescue the animal. Despite his best efforts, the horse soon slipped out of his grasp and disappeared under the broken ice. Folke barely managed to save himself and crawl to shore. The exertion sparked another serious bout of internal bleeding. The experience left him shaken and, of course, profoundly saddened.

It wasn't long before Folke's life as a cavalry officer started to become something of an anachronism. In 1923, the Life Guard Dragoons were absorbed into a modernized Swedish Army and adopted a new name — the First Cavalry Regiment. This change in structure jettisoned the old traditions of the Life Guards, and the time-honored attractions of serving in the classiest of the king's bodyguard units lost some of their glamour. As the years wore on, the group's prestige continued to erode. With the advent of tanks, cavalry units were converted into motorized infantries; between that and the seriousness of his health issues, this brave horseman and aspiring leader suddenly found himself with few occupational choices. He joined the board of the Swedish Jockey Club from 1920 to 1926 and served as its honorary treasurer. But that was hardly a role befitting a young man surrounded by successful family members with high expectations. "This was really one of the most difficult things that he had to deal with, his loss of a career," his son Bertil later recalled, "He had spent years as a military man and was forced to give it up. And he didn't really know what to do with himself next."

But his time in the cavalry had transformed him from a somewhat apathetic boy into a more decisive man with a real flair for mapping out common ground between conflicting parties. Even the Chief of Staff of the Swedish Army, General Archibald Douglas, recognized his talents, doling out rare praise for Folke's great devotion to duty, strength of character, and calm demeanor. As a dragoon, Folke had managed to be both liked and respected, earning a reputation for being an active and thoughtful listener, a skill that allowed him to easily smooth away disputes. He distinguished himself so much that his commanding officer, General Goran Gyllenstierna, advised him to consider a career in the diplomatic service. Further proof of his skills were the bronze trophies he received in 1918, 1922, and again in 1927 for the best performance in his regimental Officers' Corps. Whether he would ever have proved an outstanding fighting man no one will ever know. But, mentally, he was unflappable.

Without his illness, he might have worked hard to remain in the army. But after his health scares, his thoughts turned to safer career paths. Political events in his own country may also have influenced him: in the 1920s, Sweden began to put its policy of active neutrality into practice, playing an influential role in the Turkey-Iraq border dispute and advocating for the establishment of an organization for arbitration of international conflicts; meanwhile, Sweden and the other three Nordic states agreed to arbitrate their own differences.

During a speech about his father made in October 2011 at the University of Jordan, Bertil described the challenges and formative experiences of Folke's early career. "He chose a military career and in 1915 he joined the Life Guard Dragoons, where he developed into a good officer, caring more about others and their problems than himself. Already, during these years, he showed a talent for solving conflicts peacefully and calmly. In 1930, he was forced to relinquish his military career because of repeated intestinal bleeding, a problem he carried with him for the rest of his life," he said. And yet, life was about to present another twist, "However, before leaving the military, his uncle — the king — ordered him to present himself for duty on the French Riviera. The king was titular head of the Life Guards and as such was able to order his nephew wherever he wanted him to go. You see, this uncle had met what he considered to be a charming American couple in Nice and they had, in his view, a suitable daughter for marriage with his nephew. This daughter, as you may have surmised, became my mother."

Ever dutiful, Folke made arrangements to fulfill the king's wishes. Little did he know that a spectacular romance was about to be born.

CHAPTER THREE

A World's Fair Like No Other

In 1922, Folke Bernadotte was already 27. Since his poor health had made hash of his hopes for a long-term military career, he needed some other way to avoid becoming a social cliché. Despite a general interest in helping those in need, Folke had no clear vision of what he wanted to achieve, and this was making his uncle, King Gustaf V, antsy. Soon, the king was holding conclaves with a wide assortment of family members as to how Folke might fulfill his potential.

Eventually, they turned to Folke himself and asked him directly: What did he think he was good at? Did he want to work in finance? Did he want to work in the arts? Did he want to travel? If so, where would he want to go and why? And what about the Royal Court? If he were to be a useful member, someone pointed out, he'd have to learn multiple languages. Yes, he was proficient at German and English, but what about French? French enjoyed a long history as an international language of literature and scientific standards and was — and still is — a primary or secondary language of many international organizations.

A key component of any plan involving French included an extended break from Sweden itself, a prospect that immediately appealed to Folke. The stimulus of new surroundings might help him better contemplate his future. To learn French properly, he would, of course, have to go to Paris. But Paris, in those days, was synonymous with wine, women, and getting oneself into mischief, so the king didn't want him to go there alone. This is where Folke's worldly uncle, Prince Eugene, came in. With the older and wiser Eugene as his guide and chaperone, Folke could sample the cultural riches of the City of Light, all the while becoming more conversant in the language. So it was settled. Eugene was the perfect person to accompany Folke to France, and he was happy to do so. Fortunately, everyone was a fan of Eugene — and no one more so than Folke.

Folke later described his uncle like this: "From my earliest boyhood days, I remember how he interested himself in . . . our games. . . . He protested lively if he thought he had noticed that somebody had tried to cheat and was very insistent that the rules of the game should be followed. . . . He abhorred everything which had the least suspicion of bluff or hypocrisy and he always set store upon a person who spoke openly and boldly to his face even if what was said should prove completely contradictory to his own views. To his nephews and nieces and their children he was never Uncle Eugene but always Uncle Light (Farbror Sken in Swedish), the original reason being that it was difficult for

small children to pronounce 'Eugene.' I think that nickname
. . . is significant of his entire personality."

In Paris, Eugene didn't disappoint. At the Louvre, he
introduced Folke to the Mona Lisa and Venus de Milo, just
the appetizer course in a treasure trove filled with more than
30,000 works of art. At some of the best patisseries, he taught
him the difference between a macaron and a macaroon (the
first is meringue-based, the second is coconut-based). He
schooled him in architecture and brought to life the history
of the city as they navigated the Latin Quarter's crooked
cobblestone corridors and the palatial tree-lined boulevards
of Saint-Germain-des-Prés, a global meeting point for writers, painters, and existentialists. All the while, Folke was
picking up and perfecting his French.

They couldn't have chosen a more splendid time to be
in Paris. Following the austerity and bleakness of the First
World War, the French longed for light-heartedness. In this
unprecedented period of economic prosperity, they developed such a lust for extravagance and partying that the era
was nicknamed "Les Années Folles" or "The Crazy Years."
(The same period in the United States is frequently referred
to as the Roaring Twenties.) Cars crowded out horses and
carriages on the Parisian boulevards and rues; picture houses
opened, screening the silent films of newcomers like Jean
Renoir; and musical halls — where icons such as Josephine
Baker and Maurice Chevalier launched their careers —
became the places to see and be seen. Paris was at the heart of
it all, not only fashion and entertainment, but in the domains
of art and architecture, where movers and thinkers drew
inspiration from cubism, modernism, and neoclassicism.

The artistic ferment and still-low prices lured writers and artists from around the world including Pablo Picasso, Salvador Dalí, and James Joyce. Coco Chanel put her own perfume, Chanel No. 5, on the market in 1920 and introduced the "little black dress" in 1925. In 1924, Paris hosted the Olympic Games — at which medals were awarded for artistic in addition to sporting achievements — and it left an indelible mark on the city's architecture.

The trip opened Folke's mind and broadened his perspective, and yet it hadn't given him the clarity he so needed to plot out a viable roadmap for his future. After getting back from Paris, he filled his time by running errands for his uncle, who was genuinely impressed by Folke's work ethic and earnest desire to serve. King Gustaf V hoped his nephew could act as something of a channel between the royals and the younger generation.

But living the life of a courtier, at someone's constant beck and call, was certainly not something Folke could see himself doing for long. Soon he returned to full-time duty with his newly constructed regiment, called the Cavalry Regiment, and to the familiar round of riding, partying, and shooting that came with it. In 1927, he took off again with Prince Eugene, this time to Italy and Egypt, and then to Greece and Turkey, two countries that had been embroiled in war from 1919 to 1922. He had developed a penchant for packing up and leaving his comfort zone and experiencing new things. The months hummed along at a nice clip.

In 1928, he took yet another journey. This trip, the one his son mentioned in his speech, was one that would upend his life. At the invitation of his uncle — who was making his yearly round of the lawn tennis tournaments on the French Riviera under the pseudonym "Mr. G" — Folke traveled to the sun-splashed south of France. There, the sunny days spent on the dazzling Mediterranean coastline gave way to an ever-spinning carousel of partying and gambling at night. A center of creativity during the 1920s and 1930s, the Riviera — like Paris — exerted a gravitational pull upon artists and writers from the far reaches of the world. It was during this period on the French Riviera that F. Scott Fitzgerald finished *The Great Gatsby* and met Gerald and Sara Murphy, the glamorous couple that he would use as the inspiration for his last novel, *Tender Is the Night*.

Moored offshore of this playboy's paradise alongside several fine boats and steam yachts was the luxurious 774-foot-long *Homeric* cruising vessel. Among the wealthy and fashionable passengers on board was an American millionaire named Hiram Edward Manville and his family. The Riviera was an A-lister hotspot, so there was no shortage of rich people. Under any other circumstances, the Manville family's presence at the high society gatherings that included the Swedish Court might have barely registered. The Manvilles would have plunged into the typical whirlwind of fancy parties — and then they would have gone on their merry way without scarcely anyone giving them a second glance.

If, that is, their daughter had not been traveling with them.

The Manvilles were among those invited to a banquet given in honor of "Mr. G," and, thanks to Gustav's carefully made table assignments, Folke found himself sitting next to the millionaire's only daughter, the tall, dark Estelle Romaine Manville, aged 23. Doe-eyed and beautiful, she exuded charm and grace, and Folke was so tongue-tied he could barely form a sentence. Rather than risk saying something stupid, he allowed all the natural stiffness of a typical Swede to hold sway. Even the normally charismatic Estelle, adept at moving in high-society circles, kept verbal communication to a minimum. "I was not really at all gripped by his personality," she would later admit. "I wondered to myself whether he wasn't actually quite an ordinary and somewhat self-preoccupied gentleman."

But then the oddest thing happened. A balloon overhead suddenly burst, causing everyone to jump. It spun down slowly and plopped right onto Folke's plate, which apparently broke the ice. Folke and Estelle couldn't help but laugh. Estelle later described Folke's laughter as "special and completely irresistible . . . his face exploded in a bright and lusty laugh and I suddenly realized that he had extraordinarily blue eyes. . . . I thought for a moment I could see the spirit in his soul and in the same instant, I realized that he was a good man." Soon they were chatting away as if they'd known each other their entire lives.

Smitten, they spent day after day together, and after only two weeks, Folke proposed to Estelle and she said yes. To someone who remarked on this quick progression, Folke answered that "you've got to be a fast talker to get the best girl in the United States."

There were glaring differences in their backgrounds. Whereas Folke was a European blue blood, Estelle had grown up with clawed-their-way-to-the-top American businessmen. Her grandfather, Charles Brayton Manville, was one of the early pioneers in the asbestos industry and founded the Johns Manville Corporation, a company that became a global leader in the manufacture of such asbestos-containing products as roofing, textiles, and insulation. Estelle's father, Hiram Edward Manville, was born in Wisconsin and educated by the Milwaukee public school system. His first job, at the age of 14 in 1886, was with Northwestern Mutual Life Insurance Company, but he left shortly thereafter for Johns Manville, where the scrappy young man leapfrogged from position to position, finally making it to president in 1924. After his brother Thomas's death in 1925, he became chairman of the board at a time when the company had assets of $32 million and sales of $50 million annually. Folke had been born into wealth; Estelle came from a family of self-made money. And yet both had grown up surrounded by all the trappings of power and prestige, and were equally dedicated to giving back as much as they got. The two complemented each other.

Even though Estelle was a beautiful and intelligent woman from a fine family, their engagement might have been blocked if not for a case of mistaken identity. Folke's parents and other members of the royal family were curious about the debutante who suddenly was to become his wife and called for an investigation into the Manville family. A wave of inquiries ensued, after which Folke's family was informed that the Manvilles were listed in the Social Register — the arbiter of who counts and who doesn't — as members of what was known as the Four Hundred, or the most prestigious upper-class families of New York. This family of Manvilles was said to be one of the most ancient families in North America, arriving in the New World in the 1600s. They were also said to be descended from a prominent baron in England. The information satisfied any reservations anyone might have harbored about the Manville name.

However, this was all based on a misunderstanding. There were actually two prominent Manville families in the United States, and the one they had wrongly investigated represented old money. In fact, Estelle's family members had nothing whatsoever to do with the other Manville family. Estelle's nouveau riche family's fortune was earned the hard way. Beyond their status as the kings of asbestos, Estelle's family's only other claim to fame was that her cousin Tommy was the most frequently married man in America, having gotten hitched to 11 different women.

At the same time, Folke's loved ones weren't the only people that were curious. Hiram Manville wanted to know more about his future son-in-law's background. Hiram didn't want a lazy playboy for his daughter but rather a man he could groom to one day take over his business interests after his death. After a bit of sleuthing, Hiram learned that all of Folke's uncles and other relatives were sober, serious, brilliant, hard-working, and capable of understanding international business. He assumed that Folke, coming from the same stock, shared the same traits and would no doubt be able to make the complex financial decisions necessary when dealing with the large estate Estelle and her husband would one day inherit.

But each family was deluding itself about the other. The "wrong" Manville woman was about to embark on a life with the one member of the Swedish royal family who didn't have a head for finance. But no one figured this out until after Folke and Estelle were married. By then, it didn't matter. In no time, Miss Manville, the picture of poise, had become a royal fixture. And it was apparent to anyone who knew them that the two truly loved one another. Not only did they have chemistry, they were also compatible. Both valued family and loyalty, and they shared a sense of duty and a desire to serve others. Because of the good fortune they'd enjoyed, they believed it was their obligation to spread the wealth. Estelle's natural charisma and compassion allowed her to step right into her future royal duties.

The two married on December 1, 1928, in the small ivy-covered Episcopal Church of St. John in Pleasantville, New York, a modern suburb of New York City. According to the *New York Times*, the wedding was "one of the most brilliant society gatherings in recent years." The ceremony was at 4 p.m., meaning the sun was already beginning to set. Candles were used in place of artificial lighting to beautifully illuminate the church's interior, which "sparkled as decorations, jewels and dress uniforms flashed in the light of hundreds of candles." Wearing an elegant gown of ivory, followed by a long train bordered with seed pearls, Estelle was walked down the aisle by her father to the Bridal Chorus from Wagner's *Lohengrin*, sung by two choirs. Folke's best friend and cousin, Crown Prince Gustaf Adolf, served as best man. As was becoming the custom at this time, the always independent Estelle dropped the promise "to obey" from the ceremony. (The Anglican and Episcopal churches in Europe had voted in 1922 to remove "obey" from the wedding vows.)

Before the ceremony, Folke had presented his young bride with a small nine-pointed crown of diamonds, commissioned from the Swedish court jeweler, that Estelle balanced on top of her short brunette curls. Complementing the coronet was a veil of old Brussels lace — a costly lace known for its delicacy — that Folke had inherited from his grandmother, Queen Sophia. The bride carried a sheaf of calla lilies held together by a silk ribbon, her neck adorned with a multi-strand pearl necklace from which a bedazzling diamond and pearl pendant hung. Although only 250 of the couple's closest friends and family members attended the service, more than 2,000 admirers lined the mile-and-a-quarter route between the church and Hi-Esmarco, the Manville's spacious country estate, hoping to catch a glimpse of the happy couple. At Hi-Esmarco, a further 1,000 guests awaited the arrival of the bride and groom for their evening reception. By all accounts, the over-the-top nuptials were an event to remember, with larger-than-life canopies of fresh flowers. Even the wedding cake was six feet tall.

The American press had a field day covering the festivities, reportedly the first time a member of a European royal family had married in the United States. Other glowing epitaphs included "the greatest occurrence in American Society since the wedding of Miss Consuelo Vanderbilt with the Duke of Marlborough." The whole lavish affair was estimated to have cost some $1.75 million, although, according to Estelle herself, the price tag was a "mere" $250,000.

Before they departed on a honeymoon within the United States, the newlyweds were hosted by President Calvin Coolidge and his wife, Grace, at an elegant White House luncheon, at which Crown Prince Gustaf Adolf and other members of the Swedish royal family were in attendance. And then they all spent Christmas at Hi-Esmarco with the bride's parents. This gave Hiram the chance to formally evaluate his new son-in-law's suitability. It soon became apparent to Hiram that Folke didn't have much of a viable future — he had spent his entire adult life in the Life Guard Dragoons, riding horses and preparing for battles that everyone knew would never occur. It crossed Hiram's mind that Folke may have served in the dragoons as a way to claim a career while dodging real work.

Nevertheless, Estelle loved this man, and so her parents thought their son-in-law should at least be given the chance to prove himself in the business world. Maybe Folke had a knack for it and just didn't know it yet. Hiram firmly believed that "anybody can inherit millions. It is harder to administer them. First of all, you should learn to handle money. You should go through the mill in a bank." And so for six months, Folke went to work at Lee, Higginson & Co., an investment bank in New York, where he got a crash course in the proverbial corporate ladder as he moved from one junior-level job to another. His well-meaning friends thought the work demeaning and weren't afraid to say so. Folke shot back: "Honest work never demeaned anybody." But still, he was 35, no longer a youngster with the luxury of many years ahead of him to test the waters.

After studying American business, and not really enjoying it very much, he decided the place might be the problem and so transferred his banking studies to France. But within weeks he came up against another brick wall: his French. While it was more than adequate, it wasn't at a level where he could fully comprehend his fast-talking associates and so, at the end of 1931, he returned home to Sweden, finally settling down with his bride in his native land. Although specific details are difficult to come by, some reports point to a streak of disappointing investments during this period that also may have portended the end of his business dabblings. He had put up $200,000 to become head of an electrical power corporation formed with the inventor Baltzar von Platen, but an initiative to develop the long-distance transmission of power failed, and the company lost everything. He also funneled money into a company that marketed German machine guns. This business, too, ultimately flopped.

Folke and Estelle set up house in a 20-room villa called Dragongarden, which today is still standing as the home of the Chinese Embassy in Stockholm. Estelle had a penchant for home renovation and thought nothing of rolling up her sleeves and doing some hands-on decorating. No one would have guessed that she was a millionaire's daughter or the wife of royalty. In fact, the first party she threw there was a casual crayfish feast for the workers. Though she plunged right into her new life, and ultimately liked Sweden, Estelle — now officially named Estelle Bernadotte of Wisborg — would never get used to the long dark winters. She did, however, become proficient in Swedish and quickly won the hearts of the Bernadotte family members. In 1932, when King Gustaf V's grandson Prince Lennart caused something of a scandal by forfeiting his princely titles to ask a commoner, Karin Nissvandt, to marry him against his parents' wishes, it was Estelle who stepped in to persuade the king to give his blessing. She was even spotted shopping with the king in Nice, arm-in-arm, as they searched for a wedding gift for the couple.

After their whirlwind courtship, Folke and Estelle led a fairly quiet life for the first few years of their marriage. Folke continued to stay at least somewhat involved with the Army until 1933, when he officially retired as a major. He rode horses, picking up an array of prizes for horsemanship, and from time to time presided over the meetings of the Swedish National Shooting Association. He served on the boards of various companies. He was biding his time while looking for a suitable outlet for his humanitarian impulses.

Folke and Estelle also suffered heartache during this period. The couple had always wanted children and had four sons in fairly rapid succession. But two of them died quite young. An infant, Frederik Oscar, passed away in 1934 of an enlarged thymus gland — the main organ of the lymphatic system — while Estelle was out shopping and Folke was visiting military headquarters. Another son, Gustaf, died from a blood infection at age six, in 1936. Their two surviving sons were named Folke Jr. and Bertil, born in 1931 and 1935, respectively. These tragedies shook Folke and Estelle to their core — but also made them even more sympathetic to the challenges other families faced and more determined than ever to work personally for the relief of other people's distress.

On a sunny Sunday morning in the spring of 1933, Folke was out walking his border terrier, as he always did on the weekends, on the outskirts of Stockholm when he stumbled upon a large crowd of well-mannered boys, gathered together to celebrate an altruistic brotherhood Folke would find irresistible. He recognized a friend, Sten Thiel, and asked what was going on. Sten explained that it was a Boy Scout Rally for the entire Stockholm area and that Folke's cousin, Prince Gustaf Adolf, would be coming by shortly to open the proceedings in his capacity as chief of the Swedish Scout Union. On the spot, Folke signed up to join the Scout Union. This association led to an acquaintance with the YMCA, which had only about 6,000 members, compared with the Boy Scout Association's 14,000.

Soon, Folke was channeling time and energy into both organizations, but ultimately was more in awe of the scouts' quasi-military discipline, as well as their interest in camping in the wild. He learned everything about scouting he could, and, in 1936, he joined the staff of the Swedish Boy Scouts headquarters. In that capacity, he was able to travel the following year to Amsterdam for the World Jamboree, where he experienced the thrill of meeting the founder of the movement, Lord Robert Baden-Powell. Folke also struck up a close friendship with his wife, Lady Olave Baden-Powell, who championed the value of scouting for both boys and girls, promoting the cause in 111 countries. Soon after founding the scout movement, Baden-Powell developed a training program for prospective scout leaders. Since practical instruction in the outdoors was key, the tranquil Gilwell Park, located in the Epping Forest just outside London, was purchased specifically to serve as a venue for the courses. In 1938, Folke passed the very vigorous international Gilwell Test for Scout Leaders, which required him to know everything from first aid and navigation to animal tracking and knot-tying. As a result, he was awarded the highly coveted Wood Badge for significant achievements in leadership training. He went on to act as one of the heads of an international scout rally held at Tullgarn, the king's fishing estate south of Stockholm.

For six years, Folke served the scouting movement in a variety of ways, crisscrossing the country to recruit scouts, train leaders, and explain the benefits of the scouting movement to anyone who would listen. By the end, he had visited every one of the 32 scout centers between the Arctic Circle and the Baltic. Everywhere he went, he was a hit with the boys because he never talked down to them. Whether pitching tents or building fires, he was just as at home with them as he was at an elegant state dinner.

Between his scout work and helping raise his sons, Folke Jr. and Bertil, Folke settled into a happy routine, perhaps somewhat oblivious to the political storm clouds building over Europe. In 1933, he got his first taste of life as a diplomat when he was called upon to represent the king in America. He traveled to Chicago, a city with 200,000 Swedish immigrants at the time, to attend the Century of Progress International Exposition, a World's Fair at which a major Swedish exhibition had been mounted by Americans of Swedish descent. By the 1930s, Chicago's population had reached three million, and immigrants not only from Sweden but from other parts of Europe flocked to the city in the hopes of attaining job opportunities. The fair attracted an impressive 40 million visitors, and the Swedish exhibition was a great success. Folke was so well received that he returned to the United States the following year, and then a few years after that.

These trips served as the warm-up acts for Folke's biggest odyssey to the United States, in January 1939. With Europe on the cusp of war, the king appointed Folke to serve as commissioner-general for the Swedish Exhibit at the New York World's Fair.

The lively exposition was no place for worries about Hitler's Third Reich. The culmination of years of planning, the fair commemorated the 150th anniversary of George Washington's inauguration on Wall Street and celebrated the "World of Tomorrow," aiming to alleviate the bleak conditions of the Depression and create a vision of a brighter future. Flanked by Boy Scouts, Roosevelt opened the $160 million fair with an address that emphasized the United States' desire for a peaceful future that would see a breakdown of "many barriers of intercourse" among European nations.

More than 44 million visitors were captivated by the merry-go-round of attractions. Spread out over 1,200 acres in Queens — on the site of a former ash dump — were more than 150 exhibition pavilions divided into seven "zones": Government, Community Interests, Food, Communication and Business, Production and Distribution, Transportation, and Amusement. The gleaming white Trylon and Perisphere structures, icons of modern design symbolizing the spirit of late-1930s America, served as a glorious centerpiece. The Perisphere, a massive sphere 180 feet in diameter, was linked to the 610-foot spire-shaped Trylon by the world's longest escalator at the time. In keeping with the fair's forward-looking theme, the Perisphere housed a diorama of a utopian city of the future known as "Democracity." In the same vein, the fair gave the public its first glimpse of color photography, nylon, air conditioning, fluorescent lamps, and full-scale mechanized exhibits from business giants such as IBM, RCA, and General Electric. The Food Zone, too, showcased the latest technology and products from American companies, and promoted many brands still found on store shelves today. The exhibit for Borden's Milk featured 150 cows on a "Rotolactor" that mechanically bathed, dried, and milked them, while Coca-Cola demonstrated the inner workings of a bottling plant, and Kraft revealed how the modern pasteurization process was used for Philadelphia Cream Cheese. There were also marionette shows and thrill rides, girlie reviews and choreographed aquatic spectacles.

It was all dazzling and dramatic. But when Folke arrived, he was anything but impressed after discovering that, much to his dismay, all things Sweden had been relegated to one small hall in an inauspicious building intended to accommodate several nations. This didn't sit well with Folke or with any of the Swedes, who took great pride in their country's accomplishments, and he didn't waste any time voicing his complaints. But instead of shaking his fist, he protested quietly but sincerely. In the end, he got what he wanted — space for a grand and entirely Swedish pavilion called Swedish Square that millions would rank as one of the fair's most outstanding venues. Visitors could enjoy music, dancing, a film in a 200-seat theater, and displays of pottery, textiles, and furniture. A really big hit was the pavilion's restaurant, the Three Crowns, which featured a revolving smorgasbord full of appetizers and entrées. The person Folke had brought with him to manage it wound up staying on in the United States and opening his own Scandinavian restaurant.

Making the pavilion a success had been complicated and costly; Folke had needed to hire the right talent, and quickly. In Sweden, he had supervised a laborious process aimed at weeding out the low performers in order to uncover the true gems. An initial pool of 250 men and women, all of whom were trained and then tested, was whittled down to 50. They then sat through an intensive series of lectures that covered every aspect of Swedish history and culture so that there was no chance a visitor's question could stump them. The cream of the crop — 11 out of the 50 — were chosen to accompany Folke and the committee to New York. Folke even put great thought into what they should wear. Men and women were issued blue blazers with the three royal Swedish crowns embroidered on the pocket. The men had gray flannel trousers while the women had blue skirts to be worn on weekdays and white dresses for Sundays. Everyone got a yellow tie.

Amid the stress of this massive project, Folke suffered a severe ulcer attack a week before the fair officially opened. Somehow he managed to pull himself together long enough to oversee the opening ceremony. And it was a good thing he did. Some 300 guests had been invited, but about half of them hadn't bothered to RSVP. The seating became quite chaotic when some 100 uninvited guests suddenly showed up, many of them quite distinguished. The staff was forced to make do, serving a dinner that was anything but lavish. But Folke improvised, standing up to welcome the crowd to "a picnic." He noted that it was impossible for a person not to have a good time at a picnic. Folke had been able to think on his feet, and those who had sent him to the fair were impressed.

Once everything was up and running, Folke and Estelle embarked on a trip to the American West, where Estelle hoped her husband could finally relax. The couple visited Montana's Glacier Park, living in a "log cabin" that was more like a wooden mini-mansion. Estelle had spent vacations there as a girl, and she was keen to show Folke why she loved it. A highlight of the trip was their visit with Blackfoot leaders from a nearby reservation who officially named Folke "Ema-do-yena," or "He who is idolized by everybody." The visit included an evening of tribal dances, songs, and other spirited entertainment.

On their way back to New York, they stopped in Chicago, where they were treated like celebrities. City leaders drove the pair through the streets with a police escort, speeding, and running red lights. The ride thrilled Folke; Estelle was relieved to see his face light up with a boyish grin. When he stepped out of the car at the hotel, he even handed the doorman $10 instead of the typical $1.

These idyllic days in the United States would be the last carefree ones the Bernadottes would ever know.

CHAPTER FOUR

Two Worlds Collide

In 1939, two very different worlds were taking shape — a fanciful one and reality.

In the real world, a seismic shift in the geopolitical terrain was underway. The tremors began in the wee hours of the morning on August 24, when Soviet Foreign Minister Vyacheslav Molotov and German Foreign Minister Joachim von Ribbentrop signed a 10-year non-aggression pact that paved the way for the Nazi invasion of Poland on September 1. The Russians and the Germans agreed not to attack each other and not to support any third party that might attack either country. The agreement would remain in effect until Nazi Germany reneged on it and invaded the Soviet Union on June 22, 1941. The treaty shocked the world. The countries were bitter ideological enemies, and many had thought a war between the two to be imminent. But they had gone from sworn adversaries to allies in the space of a few months. The Molotov-Ribbentrop Pact was the first clear sign that the European balance of power established at the end of the

First World War was eroding and a new round of jockeying for position was beginning.

And then there was a world of fantasy, one in which there was no Hitler and there was no war: the escapist fantasy of the World's Fair. It would not be long before the two worlds collided. When the Molotov-Ribbentrop Pact was signed, even those who rarely scanned a newspaper couldn't help but notice the Soviets' sudden withdrawal from the fair. The Stalinist structure on U.S. soil had been designed to show off the might of the prewar Soviet Union through dioramas, a statue of Lenin, and a full-scale mock-up of the ultra-modern Mayakovskaya metro station constructed in Moscow only a year earlier. But the pavilion closed, and other countries quickly followed suit. Within a year, participants from Albania, Greece, the Netherlands, Norway, Portugal, and Yugoslavia had all broken down their exhibits and hightailed it back home, as war took priority over the sharing of ideas. After the Nazi invasion in September 1939, Polish officials draped their display in black. By the time the fair closed, in October 1940, the modernist structures that had become the symbols of the entire extravaganza, the Trylon and Perisphere, would be dismantled so that their 40 million tons of steel could be used for the war effort.

American businessmen returning from European conventions helped maintain the facade of the fantasy world by claiming, as late as in July 1939, that rumors of war on the continent were greatly exaggerated. Many average Americans believed the same, naively eager to swallow the notion that what was happening across the Atlantic was really none of America's concern. A poll taken in 1939 showed that 94 percent of Americans were opposed to getting involved. There was no reason for it, the isolationists insisted. Hitler's aggressions were in Europe's backyard, not America's. And after all, even the famous songwriters, George and Ira Gershwin, wrote that we should all "see the sun through the gray" in their theme song for the fair, titled "Dawn of a New Day." But as Folke himself later described it, "all the marvelous talk in New York about 'the world of tomorrow' sounded ironic, in fact almost grotesque. When I think of the impressions I received from my journeys in Europe, which I still recall most clearly, the tragically sharp contrast between the motto of the World's Fair and developments in Europe is especially strong."

When the fair officially opened on a sweltering Sunday in late April 1939, more than a year had already passed since Germany's annexation of Austria, and hundreds of thousands of mostly German and Austrian Jews had fled their homes and countries to escape the widening pogroms. It had already been six years since the Nazis started chipping away at Jewish citizenship by carrying out the first nationwide boycott of Jewish businesses. While the effort was not terribly success-ful, it marked the beginning of a campaign by the Nazi party to strip Jews of their freedoms — and their dignity. New laws restricting employment in the civil service to "Aryans" were put in place. Jewish government workers, including valued teachers in public schools and universities, were fired without cause. In total, more than 400 decrees and regula-tions were implemented that isolated and disenfranchised Jewish Germans during the first six years of Hitler's dicta-torship. With so many horrific events unfolding thousands of miles away in Germany, at least some of the 200,000 people who showed up on the opening day of the fair in Flushing Meadows Park must have been aware.

But the isolationist impulse remained deeply entrenched in the psyche of Americans, from well-heeled city dwellers touring the fairgrounds in Queens to dust-covered farmers coaxing crops from the western plains. President Roosevelt knew about the potential refugee crisis looming in Europe. But, cognizant of Congress's reluctance to raise existing quotas on Jewish immigration, he was not ready to risk championing the rights of oppressed European Jews. Not wanting to appear entirely unsympathetic or oblivious, however, he organized a conference to study the refugee situation. In July 1938, 32 nations sent representatives to Evian, France, where they established an Intergovernmental Committee on Refugees but failed to devise any practical solutions.

In New York tabloids, the Nazis' march across Europe competed for headlines with the frequent police raids on the fair's nudie shows. One of the pavilions, designed by artist Salvador Dalí, resembled a "fun house" in which patrons could watch as topless women swam in a glass tank against a backdrop of an erupting Mount Vesuvius. Any crackdowns by the vice squad only gave these shows more publicity — and more money. They didn't go anywhere.

Among the war headlines were those about the prospect of atomic energy. Most American physicists doubted that atomic bombs were a realistic possibility, and no official U.S. atomic energy project existed. This bothered the Hungarian-born physicist Leo Szilard, a refugee from Nazi Germany. He called on his friend, Albert Einstein, serving as chairman of the World's Fair's science advisory committee, to state his worry that the Germans would develop an atomic weapon and use it without hesitation. He asked Einstein to sign a letter explaining all of this to President Roosevelt. Warning that "uranium may turn into a new and important source of energy in the immediate future," and "extremely powerful bombs of a new type may be constructed," the letter Einstein sent in August 1939 called upon Roosevelt to make sure his administration maintained regular contact with "a group of physicists working on chain reactions in America." This prompted Roosevelt to take the first steps toward what would become the Manhattan Project, a large U.S. government program to create atomic weapons. Roosevelt set up the Advisory Committee on Uranium to evaluate how far the U.S. had progressed with regard to uranium research and to recommend what role the government should play.

Then, without warning, the German armed forces, or Wehrmacht, invaded neighboring Poland from the west on September 1, 1939 — five months after the opening of the World's Fair — while the Russians stepped in to grab their share of Poland from the east. Hitler had been planning the blitzkrieg since 1933. And, as Hitler had correctly predicted, Europe's other powers were reluctant to intervene in time to help. Two days later, on September 3, Britain and France declared war on Germany in honor of their Defensive Alliance with Poland. But it would be another eight months before those countries engaged in all-out war with the Nazis. Although the poorly equipped Polish military fought bravely, holding the Nazis off for weeks, in the end, it hadn't been strong enough to resist. The battle for Poland only lasted about a month.

Two months later, on October 31, 1939, the first of two seasons of the fair was drawing to a close. An editorial in the *New York Times* said that "A year in which the World of Today seemed to be going from bad to worse might not have seemed a good year in which to hold a World's Fair celebrating the World of Tomorrow. But the New York World's Fair . . . was well-timed. It showed how comfortable a dwelling place the earth could be if men could only learn to work together. . . . In war and peace, prosperity and depression, scientific knowledge marches on. . . . But it was clear, even at the fair, that mankind has lagged behind in what have been called the social inventions. Above all, we have not yet invented a cure for war or a panacea for those destructive economic policies which preceded the present conflict."

Folke, as the Swedish commissioner general at the fair, faced a dilemma. As he later wrote, "I and the other Swedes, who were working at the Exhibition, naturally wanted to go home. I was, moreover, an officer and even though the future course of events seemed incredibly uncertain, it was my duty as a soldier to be home in Sweden in case my country should become drawn into the war. But my duty was also to remain where I was until after the Exhibition's end on Nov. 1 in order to close down the Swedish Pavilion."

After consulting with his employer, the Swedish government, Folke decided he would return home with Estelle on December 6 via Lisbon, aboard the *American Clipper*, one of the largest aircraft of the time. When this decision was taken, the war was making many Swedes uneasy, but most were still under the illusion that their foes could be kept at bay. That changed on November 30, 1939, when the realities of Hitler's intentions landed squarely on Sweden's doorstep. On that day, very early in the morning, the Soviet Union attacked Finland by land, sea, and air, without even so much as a declaration of war beforehand. The attack was in response to Finland's refusal to cede territory near the border to the Soviets. Although the Soviets boasted three times as many troops and 100 times as many tanks, the highly motivated Finnish army put up an admirable defense, holding off the Soviet advance at every turn. The David-and-Goliath story captured the world's imagination. President Roosevelt quickly extended $10 million in credit to Finland, noting that the Finns had been the only nation to pay back its war debt to the United States in full after the First World War.

The battle for Finland changed Bernadotte's plan. Right before he and Estelle were set to depart, he received a Western Union telegram from a group of leading Swedish citizens requesting he stay in America so that he could organize a volunteer corps of Scandinavian-Americans to join in Finland's struggle to repel the Soviet invaders. He also was called on to raise a fighting fund of $20 million from American financiers to support the corps and to send material aid to the fierce but underfunded Finns. It was a desperate venture, riddled with political landmines and offering little chance of success. Even Folke's American wife made clear her dismay. But Folke being Folke — a man always ready to serve — he accepted the proposition and put himself at his country's disposal. Like many Swedes, he felt an affinity for the Finns and took to heart the slogan "Finland's cause is ours." He called Swedish government officials to ensure they were on board with the project, and they were.

On February 19, 1940, Sweden's King Gustaf V publicly rejected pleas from Finland's government for Sweden to intervene in what came to be known as the Winter War. There was no other option. Otherwise Sweden's cherished neutrality would have had to be recast. But the king wasn't the head of government, so his word wasn't the final one when it came to Swedish foreign policy. The government, under Prime Minister Per Albin Hansson, had something different in mind. Even though a formal intervention couldn't be announced, a secret military aid program under the title "volunteers" was put in place. In the end, Finland's reliance on Sweden for military assistance would prove invaluable. No formal declaration of war was ever made, but Sweden was very much at its neighbor's side against the Soviet Union.

The next three months were a whirlwind for Bernadotte. It began with a trip to Washington, D.C., to gauge the political appetite for his new assignment. President Roosevelt's advisor on European affairs threw up the first roadblock when he informed Folke that it was prohibited under U.S. law to recruit soldiers in the United States to fight on foreign soil. Folke relayed the news to Swedish government officials, who agreed that the better course of action then was to focus on funding so the Finnish army might buy the airplanes and equipment it so sorely needed. But the Finnish Air Force also needed experienced pilots, so Folke tried to recruit qualified volunteers from various countries. At first, he encountered only tepid enthusiasm for the idea, but eventually he found an ally in Lord Lothian, the British Ambassador to America at the time. Lothian said that if

Folke could get the pilots to Canada, he would grant them visas to travel to England so that they could go on to Finland via Sweden. Folke managed to secure a number of planes and even reached out to Winston Churchill, who agreed to place a certain number of English planes at Finland's disposal so long as Folke was able to amass the necessary pilots and ground crews.

Folke then set forth on a lecture tour, canvassing the country to raise money by pleading Finland's case. He was accompanied by the famous Swedish nurse and philanthropist Elsa Brändström, who had made her name in European relief work after the First World War. Brändström was highly regarded for her efforts to create a German home for children orphaned by the war. Folke was thrilled to have such a well-respected humanitarian by his side. But it wasn't long before his delight was overshadowed by a brouhaha involving Russian media working in America. The *Daily Worker* had come out with a sensational headline, "Nephew of King of Sweden Agent of Mannerheim," claiming that Folke was working undercover for the commander-in-chief of Finnish Armed Forces, Carl Mannerheim. Investigating where the story came from, Folke discovered that some of the men who had visited him under the pretense of enlisting as volunteer pilots were actually communist spies trying to glean details about his plans. They had produced forged credentials, purporting to have seen active duty as volunteers in South American revolutions. Folke was angry with himself for failing to detect that they were imposters, especially since they had never clearly stated how they'd heard of his mission. The incident sparked an embarrassing amount of attention from

American newspapers that then closely tracked Bernadotte's comings and goings.

Despite the distractions, Folke was able to raise enough money in America for the manning of ambulances and military equipment for Finland. Satisfied with his accomplishments, he set sail for Europe on the transatlantic liner *Conte de Savoia*. He was headed home. After a week's journey, he reached Paris, where a telegram from New York was waiting for him at his hotel. He learned that his efforts on Finland's behalf had borne fruit — he was only 10 pilots short of filling the available planes. The British Embassy promised these men could easily be recruited among temporarily inactive Polish airmen in Britain. Bernadotte was elated that he'd done his country proud by successfully completing the difficult task he'd been given.

But the next morning, on March 13, 1940, one look at the Paris newspapers turned his mood upside down. The headlines announced that a treaty had been signed between Finland and the Soviet Union the day before. This should have been good news. But although the 105-day Winter War was over, the treaty had cost Finland dearly. The country was forced to cede the equivalent of a tenth of its territory, including the key cities of Vyborg, Sortavala, and Käkisalmi — more land than the Soviets had initially demanded before the war. It also struck a blow to Bernadotte, whose work — as it turned out — had been almost entirely in vain. His spirits sunk, he called New York with instructions to discontinue the operation immediately. He was glad the war had come to an end, but he wished he could have done more to help the Finns — and sooner. He found himself utterly adrift again, with no concrete plans for the future.

As he returned to Stockholm at the end of March, he felt a deep sense of disappointment. Despite months of hard work, he had almost nothing to show for his travels beyond a list of personal contacts he'd made in America. But he had little time to wallow in self-pity. Within a few weeks, German warships entered major Norwegian ports, occupying the country even though it had declared itself neutral, and German forces also took control of Copenhagen and other Danish cities. The invasion of Denmark and Norway marked a catastrophic turning point. No longer could this be called a "Phony War." This was the real start of an all-too-real war in Western Europe. Hitler wanted access to Norway's extensive coastline, and he got it. Immediately, all Swedish military officers were called up. Folke presented himself at his regiment but as a man now in his mid-40s, he was deemed too old to do active duty as a soldier. Instead, he was placed at the foot of a fortuitous precipice when his superiors presented him with a new challenge. The military was pulling together a special unit that would be responsible for the care of military personnel from hostile countries who might end up interned in Sweden.

Because Sweden had a strict official policy of neutrality, the country was becoming an important refuge for the crews of damaged aircraft from both sides of the war, especially as it was located in the middle of the action. As European hostilities crept closer to Sweden, the number of internees shot up. Already, in September 1939, Sweden had been forced to take charge of 169 Polish sailors after they escaped by submarine to Sweden's east coast. Then, in the early months of 1940, Danish and British military personnel began flooding into Sweden. By the end of that year, some 5,000 men of various nationalities were being interned, all of whom required food, clothing, healthcare, accommodation, and supervision. This created something of a logistical nightmare for authorities, and so a senior Swedish officer named Axel Rappe tapped Folke for the job of overseeing it. It was a colossal assignment and no doubt an onerous one. Not only was he to manage the internment camps, but he also was responsible for entertaining the men and providing a safe haven until they could be returned to their own countries. Folke didn't hesitate to accept.

Whether he knew it or not, Folke was stepping into a minefield. In 1941, Operation Barbarossa — the code name for the Axis invasion of the Soviet Union that started on June 22, 1941 — left a number of Russian servicemen interned in Sweden. That year also saw the arrival of more than 1,500 American airmen, mostly members of U.S. Army Air Force crews who had been on damaged B-17 and B-24 bombers. Unlike civilian refugees from Germany, who were kept in internment camps, British and American airmen were treated more like tourists on a pleasant holiday, with stays arranged in hotels and bed and breakfast establishments, mostly in the picturesque Falun area in central Sweden. Not only did they enjoy the ability to move about at will, but they also received their regular military pay from their home countries, which left them much better off economically than even Swedish residents. This didn't sit so well with the locals. It was Folke's job, therefore, to ease the tensions. The best he could do was to keep the parties separate from one another as much as possible. The Russians posed a different kind of problem for Folke, as many of them didn't want to be repatriated to their home country — they wanted to stay in Sweden permanently.

At the time, internment was regulated by a system of rules — the Geneva Conventions — that governed the treatment of prisoners of war and civilian enemy nationals, including diplomats. But according to Folke, these regulations were extremely vague, with many details open to interpretation. Certain clauses gave the authorities a lot of leeway when it came to how much freedom of movement internees could have. Again, the Swedish public was asking questions. Why were some internees given special treatment? The foreign legations, too, wanted to know why all internments weren't created equal. The Americans and English were billeted in much more desirable environs, where they walked around freely, while the Russian, German, and Polish internees were roughing it in rustic housing under close eye in well-guarded camps. (In fact, the Russian authorities urged Folke to follow that policy for their citizens because they didn't want them mingling with the Swedish population or anyone from the West.) In view of the Swedes' strong enmity toward the Germans confined there, Folke also believed it wise to restrict them to camp areas. Folke may have been in charge officially, but he was serving many masters.

In addition to handling thousands of internees, Folke was named head of the Swedish Army Education Corps, charged with providing opportunities for distraction to some 400,000 Swedish men at arms. Toward that end, he secured films, books, and even the ability to take vocational courses — all nice diversions for men under a great deal of stress.

Then came the summer of 1941. Having already obtained permission a year earlier to move troops on leave through Sweden on their way to and from occupied Norway, Germany now escalated its demands, asking to move an entire division, including its equipment, through Sweden from occupied Norway to Finland. For Sweden to refuse would be virtual suicide. There were only 40,000 Swedes under arms — and they were no match for the mighty German military machine. The country would be decimated, and the loss of lives greater than anyone dared consider. Yet to allow passage would draw the ire of so many other countries. Even worse, the haven of safety would be wiped away, and Leningrad, among other places, would likely fall quickly because of the ease of attack through Sweden. Even those Americans who had harbored an isolationist fantasy had to face a dark and foreboding reality that summer. With Hitler gaining ground, they could no longer cling to the fiction of neutrality.

The Swedish king was unsure what to do. Crown Prince Gustaf Adolf had married two Englishwomen over the years, and even preferred to speak English in his home. Folke was married to an American and felt very much at ease in the West. The king was inclined to lean away from meeting German demands. But many Swedes believed, at least for the first years of the war, that cooperation with Germany was a necessary evil in order to preserve a delicate neutrality. After all, there was no English Channel separating Sweden from the German armies in Norway and Finland, and the country was pretty much defenseless against the powerful Luftwaffe.

Perched on Germany's northern flank, Sweden found itself in a precarious position. Was it supposed to acquiesce to these orders in the face of overwhelming force and thus become a satellite? Or was it to deny transit to the Germans and therefore take a suicidal stand in support of the West? Swedish Prime Minister Per Albin Hansson, who would become known for his appeasement stance, tried to make Sweden's intentions clear with a catchphrase: "Friendly with all other nations, and strongly linked to our neighbors, we look on no one as our enemy." And yet this was a frightening period for the country and for the Bernadottes. Folke found himself involved in matters he'd never before come upon as a member of the royal family. For the first time, he was faced with the fear that everything he had known all his life might suddenly disappear forever. His country could be crushed, the king imprisoned — or worse. His wife, his children, his countrymen — no one was safe.

Backed into a corner, Sweden reached a compromise with Germany. A single German division, but no more, would be allowed to pass through Sweden — enough that the Allies were irate over the act, but not significant enough to shift the course of the war. And yet there's no denying that during this period Sweden's image took on a darker hue as the country put its considerable assets at Germany's disposal. Between 1940 and 1943, Stockholm allowed more than 650,000 Nazi soldiers to cross Swedish territory to reach Germany's occupied Nordic neighbors. But no such permission was granted to the Allies. Later, to counter its image as a neutral with only its own interests at heart, Sweden would initiate humanitarian actions for thousands of victims of Nazi aggression, which helped to remove much of the stigma of collaboration. And a lot of that behavior would be instigated by Folke, whose mantra was that Sweden should always help those in need.

Altogether, about 12,000 internees passed through Bernadotte's care. Folke's taste of so much responsibility only made him hungry for more. And he got it. By Christmas 1942, it had become obvious that the 83-year-old chairman of the Swedish Red Cross, Prince Carl, would need someone to take over his duties. With Germans becoming more and more maniacal, Sweden still stood a good chance of being invaded. The demands that would be placed on the Swedish Red Cross would be extraordinary and too much for Folke's elderly uncle to handle. Even if Sweden escaped occupation, the Red Cross would be called upon to help other Scandinavian countries restore their standard of living after the war.

The search for a successor was on. By the latter part of 1942, serious discussions were underway as to how to fill the void. The highly respected Red Cross worker Lieutenant General Axel Hultkrantz suggested to Sigfrid Edström, director of the huge ASEA electric concern, chairman of the International Olympic Committee and one of the most prominent figures in Sweden, that Folke take over. Edström agreed with the choice: "No better man than Folke Bernadotte can the Red Cross find," he said. "I saw how he managed the Swedish effort in the New York World Fair. But I fear we shall never get him. He is a much sought-after man." But a proud Prince Carl relayed the request himself to his nephew, and at the annual general meeting of the Swedish Red Cross, Folke accepted the post of vice-chairman "with gratitude, pleasure, and enthusiasm." Sven Grafström, the Swedish diplomat and diarist, noted in his journal, "The Swedish-American Society, along with many other organizations, held a big dinner at the Grand Hotel [in Stockholm]. Folke Bernadotte presided and gave a very good welcoming speech. He gives a much more energetic and intelligent impression than his royal cousins."

As Folke later wrote, he felt a deep respect for the humanitarian ideals of the Red Cross and for its great tradition. Even if the aim of the Swedish Red Cross was primarily to be of service to its own country, the venerable organization, founded in 1865, was an integral part of a significant international body. And Carl had distinguished himself as the president of one of the largest and best organized of its divisions, earning several Nobel Peace Prize nominations for his accomplishments.

Folke's first move was to draw up a sequence of steps for the Swedish Red Cross so the organization could jump into action the minute an armistice was signed. Toward that end, Folke connected with similar relief agencies in other countries to find out how they might join forces for the greater good. Of all the challenges before him, one opportunity for the Swedish Red Cross to make a difference rose above the rest: the assistance of prisoners of war. It was the most pressing need at hand, and Folke's background with internees made him more sensitive to their plight. Folke saw the detainment of hundreds of thousands of prisoners of war as a "crime against humanity."

Soon he would get the chance to do something about it. In October 1943, Folke directed the first — and one of the most unique — prisoner exchanges involving German and Allied prisoners of war. Sweden was becoming a more outward-looking country, increasingly proactive in humanitarian relief. Folke, too, took a leap onto the international stage. But it would not go smoothly for Sweden, or for Folke. The pacifist nation would be harshly chastised for helping the Nazis. Folke also would find himself disparaged for fraternizing with the enemy.

CHAPTER FIVE

A Colossal Effort

Three days before Christmas in 1943, a U.S. Army sergeant named Howard Thornley, a 19-year-old from Minneapolis with floppy brown hair and deep-set eyes, was returning to his base at Bassingbourn, England, following a bombing run on Osnabrück, a city in northwest Germany, when his B-17 took fire from Nazi fighter aircraft over German-occupied Holland. The gunner in one of the Flying Fortress's ball turrets was killed, and the plane's right wing caught fire. The crew struggled to extinguish the blaze, but Thornley and the others knew it was only a matter of minutes before the gas tank exploded. The pilot yelled for everyone to bail out. Flying at nearly 25,000 feet over heavy cloud cover, they had no idea if they were above land or water. Thornley and eight other crew members took a white-knuckle high dive out the door and somehow managed to parachute safely to the ground. Although widely scattered, all were quickly rounded up, with Thornley held in a small village by a group of Dutch civilians until a German soldier could arrive by bicycle from a nearby town.

Thornley spent a week in solitary confinement in Amsterdam before being transported to an interrogation center in Frankfurt, where he was questioned six times by two German officers who spoke perfect English. One had lived in Denver for 18 years before the war; the other was originally from Philadelphia. Thornley gave up the requisite name, rank, and serial number, but nothing else. His resolve was unnecessary, though. They already knew everything about him. What high school he attended. The Air Force base where he trained. Even the dates. It was clear, Thornley recalled later, that the Germans had a spy at his base in England. Such information could only have come from his official military record. One of his tormentors was a German officer sporting a Red Cross armband who tried to play the role of genteel father figure and offered to let Thornley's parents know he was alive. When the young sergeant remained silent, Thornley later recalled, the man erupted. "How can I notify your parents if you do not tell me your bomb load?" he screamed. "My superiors will not be pleased."

The debrief complete, Thornley was then packed into a tiny boxcar with dozens of other prisoners and shunted off to the picturesque rolling hills outside Krems, Austria, and the den of misery known as Stalag 17-B. After four days and nights without water, the prisoners arrived at what appeared to be a small, flat city. More than 100,000 prisoners lived in and around dozens of low-slung barracks surrounded by guard towers and razor wire, 40,000 of them in the stalag itself and another 60,000 or so outside the camp, assigned to work details on nearby farms and factories. The men, most of them enlisted, were from all corners of Europe, and housed according to nationality. The Poles had arrived first, when the camp was little more than a collection of tents with straw strewn about for flooring, but others had trickled in as the Nazi tanks rolled across Europe in 1940 and 1941 — French, Dutch, and Belgians first, then Serbs and Russians. The Americans began arriving in late 1943, many of them as transferees from other camps, but more and more of them from downed aircraft as the autumn wore on. By the time Thornley arrived, there were about 4,400 Americans at Stalag 17-B.

The barracks occupied by the Americans were left over from the First World War and were never heated, making those first few winter months nearly unbearable. Many prisoners developed chilblains due to repeated exposure to the cold, which caused itching, swelling, and blistering on their feet. At night, fleas would feed on the cracks in the men's red, swollen skin. Once, Thornley had a wisdom tooth pulled without any painkiller. Another time, he vomited for three days straight. Almost everyone was plagued by stomach issues. All Thornley and the others could do was wait and wait — and hang on. Every prisoner was desperate to know what was going on in the outside world. Radios were forbidden, although some of the men housed with Thornley had homemade crystal sets and were able to hear BBC newscasts. When the Germans caught wind of this, though, they tore the barracks to pieces and confiscated the receivers. From then on, the prisoners' every move was monitored. If anyone dared try to escape the compounds, surrounded by double rows of barbed-wire fencing, the helmeted Nazi guards with machine guns manning the towers at the edges of the camp would shoot to kill. Back in Minnesota, Thornley's family had no idea what had happened to him. His mother didn't receive word of his capture for more than a year. She was certain he was dead.

As the weeks and months dragged on, Thornley and his fellow prisoners survived on small slabs of bread and hardtack often infested with some kind of tiny black insect no one could identify. Occasionally, a bowl of thin, watery, lukewarm "soup" with white cabbage worms floating on its scummy surface was placed before them. Every few months or so, each prisoner received a special treat: a horse meat patty. "We learned never to look at what we were eating," Thornley said in a 1983 interview with author Larry Scholl. By March 1945 — when the Germans forced the prisoners on a days-long march into the woods to escape the incoming Russians — Thornley weighed less than 100 pounds. Two months later, when the prisoners were finally freed by American troops and flown in C-47s to Nancy, France, he was nothing but skin and bones.

The food served at every camp was never enough to sustain a life. But there was one thing that kept Thornley and the other prisoners going: parcels from the Red Cross. It's safe to assume that many more of the 1.4 million American and Allied prisoners of war in Germany and elsewhere would have perished were it not for those packages. Some of the men had spent as long as five years in barbed wire worlds, "waiting on winning," as one POW newsletter described the experience. Gross malnutrition was rampant, leading a few of the men to lose their sight. The only reason so many POWs were able to return home alive was because of the more than 27 million parcels prepared and shipped by the American Red Cross to the International Red Cross in Geneva for distribution in the camps. Most of the goods were non-perishables such as cheese, prunes, coffee, canned tuna, and corned beef; each parcel weighed about 11 pounds. Christmas packages included extras such as jam, honey, deviled ham, chewing gum, and pictures of American scenery.

"Our Red Cross parcels were vital to us. Sometimes we didn't receive any for two or three months. Other times we might get one a week for a while," Thornley said. "The gaps were because the Germans took so many for themselves. Later, on our forced march, we saw much evidence of this.... Passing near homes, we would see canned items from American parcels in windows. Few of us would have lived through this had it not been for the Red Cross parcels."

The International Red Cross's official mission from its founding in Geneva in 1863 was the care of victims in times of war. But its role expanded exponentially during the First World War, when it established an agency focused exclusively on prisoners of war. By the end of the war, the Red Cross had distributed about 1.9 million parcels and had helped negotiate the exchange and safe repatriation of 200,000 prisoners. The International Committee of the Red Cross did such an admirable job that the Nobel Committee awarded it the 1917 Peace Prize, the first of three Nobel prizes the Red Cross would win.

The Second World War would require an even greater effort from the organization. When the Germans attacked

Poland in 1939, more than half a million Polish soldiers were captured in just 22 days. It fell to the Red Cross to compile and collate all the information about them. German attacks on the Netherlands, Belgium, Luxembourg, and France in the spring of 1940 added 30,000 to the roster of foreigners, British troops among them, taken prisoner by the Germans and in need of assistance. And then there were the hundreds of thousands of civilian refugees left lost and homeless following the German rampages. Day after day, Red Cross officials were bombarded with frantic and heartbreaking inquiries as to the whereabouts and health of loved ones. By the time the war was over, the Red Cross would make 12,750 official visits to different POW camps across the globe, usually in the form of trained medical staff who checked on the prisoners' health, living quarters, and quality of food. Complaints about the way POWs were treated were made to Red Cross officials who then passed them on to the relevant authorities. The agency also enabled communication between families and prisoners, ultimately passing on more than 120 million messages to recipients in 41 countries.

While volunteers for the world's largest humanitarian organization wore many hats, one of their most important assignments was negotiating for the exchange and release of seriously wounded and sick soldiers, always a dicey proposition. Before Folke Bernadotte entered the picture as vice-president of the Swedish Red Cross in 1943, the International Red Cross's efforts in that area had been woefully lacking. Early in the war, in 1940, there had been an exchange of hundreds of invalids between Germany and France, before the latter's capitulation, and later there were occasional swaps of seriously wounded British and Italian prisoners and medical personnel aboard hospital ships. But the most ambitious effort before 1943 to organize a large-scale exchange of prisoners of war between Britain and Germany failed spectacularly.

Months of negotiation and meticulous planning had been devoted to the effort. Ever since 1940, the Red Cross had been inching its way along the slow and unpredictable path toward securing the exchange of 3,000 prisoners. Each camp had compiled a list of those who might be eligible for repatriation on medical grounds, lists that then had to be rubber-stamped by the camp's German Commandant. Next, these repatriation candidates had to plead their case before a Mixed Medical Commission, usually made up of two people from a neutral country and one from the detaining power.

British bombardier Cyril Rofe, an RAF sergeant shot down in June 1941 and badly wounded in the process, tried all manner of means of escape from his German captors, including an appearance before one of the medical commissions. "Anybody who had the slightest chance was sent up before them to try his luck. I was told that I had no hope of getting through, but that I might as well have a crack at it. Some Swiss and German doctors sat at a table," he said. "My arm was still in plaster and I stood there trying to look weak and helpless, while the Commission examined a most imposing array of X-ray photographs. They were most sympathetic and I was having visions of myself back in England when one of them suddenly looked at my papers. 'Flieger,' he said. The members of the panel smiled sadly and shook their heads."

As a Flieger, or aviator, Rofe wasn't going anywhere. The Germans weren't about to risk Rofe ending up back in the air.

Once the medical formalities were completed and the go-ahead for an exchange of approved POWs was given, repatriates had to be transported and assembled at convenient, agreed-upon points, usually places with access to a quality medical facility. The one thing all parties could subscribe to was the best way to repatriate large numbers of sick soldiers: it had to be by ship and in the care of medical orderlies also being repatriated. Then they could be taken by hospital trains to various designated ports, where they could be transferred to hospital ships headed for their home countries. In the case of this particular repatriation deal, all parties settled on the ports of Newhaven in England and Dieppe in Normandy. The swap was to happen during the daylight hours between October 4 and 7, 1941 — at a time when the tides were in their favor. Initially, everything seemed to be going according to the script. Groups of badly wounded but ecstatic British soldiers were transferred in mid-September from their hospitals to Dieppe, and, on the other side of the channel, a group of hopeful Germans waited to embark for home on British ships.

Then, on September 20, the Germans changed their tune. Although the deal had been on the table for months, they wanted to revisit the terms. They were no longer willing to turn over 1,500 wounded British prisoners for only a few dozen Germans. Instead, they wanted to start the negotiation process all over again. The stakes were enormous and the British tried to appease the Germans. But on October 6, with time running out, the Nazis issued an unexpected ultimatum. They would accept nothing less than a one-to-one-exchange ratio. The demand was in blatant violation of the terms of the Geneva Conventions, which said nations had to repatriate any prisoners of war who were seriously wounded or ill, without regard for numbers. The British government stood firm, and the sailing of the ships was called off just hours before they were scheduled to depart. The hopes of the British and German prisoners were dashed, and they found themselves on their way back to camps they had hoped never to set foot in again.

One of the British soldiers, Geoff Griffin, who nearly lost an arm after his capture in France, spoke for many when he later described his devastation. "I suppose most of us had experienced some disappointments in life, but at that moment there could not have been a more dejected lot of men than us. We slunk back to the barracks and I know that I cried my eyes out; many of my comrades did the same."

Against a backdrop of the earlier fiasco, it is understandable that newly minted Red Cross official Folke Bernadotte wanted to demonstrate that the Swedes could succeed where others failed. A new exchange effort was scheduled for 1943, this time on Swedish soil.

In Folke's mind, the Swedish Red Cross's duties could be divided into three categories: to care for suffering populations within the Scandinavian peninsula; to perform relief work among the German population in the event of a Nazi defeat; and to oversee the exchange of POWs. A small organization with a limited budget, the Swedish Red Cross focused mostly on domestic issues in times of peace. But in wartime it could become a useful instrument of Sweden's foreign policy and help boost Sweden's stature in the world. Toward the end of the First World War, Folke's predecessor in the post, Prince Carl, had led the organization in a massive operation to care for and eventually exchange thousands of Russian and German prisoners of war. Now it was Folke's turn to ramp up his profile on a more impactful stage. Although preliminary negotiations for the proposed 1943 exchange had been handled by the International Red Cross in Geneva, working closely with the Swiss government, Folke and the Swedish Red Cross had been tapped to oversee the technical details. First on the to-do list was to arrange a series of conferences at which the two main stakeholders — Britain and Germany — could come to an agreement on terms for the exchange.

Fortunately, Folke and his compatriots were in a much better position to succeed relative to the botched exchange in 1941. Although Europe was mired in violence, and the Final Solution to the Jewish Question — die Endlösung der Judenfrage in German — was in full swing, the Germans were on the defensive in 1943. And they were exhausted. The tides of war had shifted toward the Allies.

In the east, the Battle of Stalingrad, a five-month showdown that started in August 1942, had demoralized the Germans. More than 2 million soldiers and Soviet civilians died in what is now regarded as the largest and bloodiest single battle in the history of human warfare. The city was decimated by the early German assault and subsequent pullback of Russian forces, but the invaders were later encircled and slowly starved in positions over the course of two months. Despite Hitler's insistence that they stay and fight to the death, the entire German 6th Army surrendered to the

Soviets. The Nazis would never fully recover, and the battle marked the beginning of the Soviet advance to Berlin.

Just weeks later on May 7, 1943, to the south, the British 7th Armoured Division took control of Tunis, the capital of Tunisia, and the U.S. Army Corps captured Bizerte on the Mediterranean coast, the only port in North Africa that was still in Axis hands. Six days later, on May 13, 1943, the Axis forces in North Africa suffered 40,000 casualties in Tunisia alone. The troops surrendered, and 267,000 German and Italian soldiers became prisoners of war. The campaign for North Africa was over. An Allied invasion of Sicily and Italy followed, and Mussolini's government fell in July 1943, though Allied forces continued to fight Germans in Italy until 1945. The Third Reich was considerably weakened and, for the first time, there were more Germans in captivity than Allied personnel (excluding Soviets). The decisive losses chipped away at German bravado, and the Nazis became much more accommodating negotiators when it came time to push for an exchange of POWs.

Closer to home, the waning of Germany's power brought new pitfalls. In occupied Denmark, Danes learned of the German setbacks via an underground press and Swedish and English radio broadcasts. Denmark had remained relatively calm until then, with the Danish government left standing even after the German invasion on April 9, 1940. But the Danes harbored centuries-old hostilities toward the Germans, and the occupation had brought those emotions roiling to the surface. With German troops and police, their behavior was deliberately standoffish and frosty: the Danish "cold shoulder" became famous. But they began to increase their resistance during the spring of 1943, and by summer, tensions reached a boiling point and sparked rioting and strikes, which prompted the Germans to proclaim a state of emergency on August 29. A few weeks later, the Germans fired a new salvo, rounding up the Jews, who had to that point been relatively unscathed in Denmark, and deporting them to Germany. However, by then most of the 7,000 Danish Jews had already escaped to Sweden or gone into hiding with the help of non-Jewish Danes.

With the Nazis hobbled, the scene was finally set in the fall of 1943 for a propitious exchange of POWs. After two years of tense negotiations, a play-by-play arrangement had been worked out: this time the exchanges would happen in the Swedish port city of Gothenburg, as well as through Smyrna, Turkey, and Oran, Algeria.

With the Swedish Red Cross handling most of the technicalities, Folke finally had a chance to test his old-fashioned military moxie on a grand scale. As Folke later wrote, a number of ships, from both England and Germany, were at his disposal, and it wasn't long before he fully appreciated the scope of the task ahead of him. "I do not know how many times my assistants and I drafted detailed plans for a transport and exchange program — plans that could not be carried out the following day for various reasons. It happened that at the last minute a few of the assigned ships were torpedoed or bombed. So we had to start all over again," he said. "We did this with enthusiasm. For my own part, I can say that until then, I had never had a mission which interested me more. The consciousness of being a cog in a machine which would enable thousands of soldiers of various nationalities to be sent back to their homeland after many years of imprisonment filled us with great happiness, and encouraged us to do our utmost to make everything run smoothly."

The prisoners and medical staff were asked to board two German steamships, the *Meteor* and the *Ruegen*, docked in the German port of Swinemünde. Prisoners who were not completely immobile traveled separately, via the German port city of Sassnitz and the Swedish harbor city of Trelleborg on ferries, enjoying the special perk of staying in cabins with stewards to wait on them. It was quite a change from the cold, lice- and flea-infested quarters they were used to. British solider Geoff Griffin was among this first repatriation group. "It is difficult to explain our feelings about what was happening but having all had a luxuriating bath and a shave, we were ushered into a large cabin where a table was set with all sorts of cold meats, potatoes and salad, and we all immediately set to and tucked into the meal," Griffin later recalled. "We did not realize how small our stomachs had become so we could not do complete justice to the meal, although we were really hungry."

Arriving in Gothenburg days later, the soldiers that had lived years in the dark couldn't help but gawk at the twinkling lights of the port. They were dazzling. As they disembarked the Swedish ship, they each received something of a treasure cache from the Red Cross: a box brimming with fruits, matches, chocolates, cigarettes, and other much-appreciated items.

En route to another vessel, they crossed paths with the wounded German soldiers for whom they had been exchanged. Some traded pleasantries. The Allied soldiers were then transported on the SS *Drottningholm* from Gothenburg to Liverpool. "The troops were unanimous in expressing their delight at the reception given to them by all the Swedes whom they saw or met," a member of the British Legation in Stockholm said. "They were the object of enthusiastic demonstrations the whole way from Trelleborg to Gothenburg and the press was full of photographs and sympathetic anecdotes. To me the most poignant memory is of a Swedish band on the quayside playing 'Home Sweet Home' with hundreds of our soldiers hanging over the sides of the two big liners singing not boisterously but from the bottom of their hearts."

In total, about 10,000 invalid prisoners of war were exchanged between Britain and Germany, some of whom had been in enemy hands for as long as four years. In every port they pulled into, a brass band was standing by to welcome the troops with a rousing medley of "It's a Long Way to Tipperary" and other wartime standards. The loudest reactions from the crowds gathered to greet them were reserved for the soldiers carried out on stretchers.

From registering and caring for thousands of exhausted and disoriented soldiers to engaging the brass band to play, Folke had skillfully and successfully stage-managed every key detail of the venture. In Gothenburg, he stood on the quay, looking distinguished in his neatly pressed Red Cross uniform, and took stock of the results of his hard work. Members of his large team, also donning crisp Red Cross uniforms, were assigned to feed, check in, and give medical assistance to the prisoners of war coming at them from opposite ends of the front. It was a proud moment for Folke and for the Red Cross. It was also the first time most Americans heard both Folke's name and his voice on their airwaves.

On October 20, 1943, an NBC News broadcast from aboard the hospital ship *Atlantis*, in Gothenburg, carried this report by correspondent David Anderson: "As I came on this ship less than a half hour ago, wounded German soldiers were being disembarked on stretchers. . . . Before she leaves port, she will have on board somewhere around 8,000 British wounded or protected personnel who will be repatriated. Her Red Cross flag is as good an assurance as any ship can have in these days of total war that she'll arrive safely back in port. . . . The man responsible for the arrangements in Sweden is Count Folke Bernadotte, the vice-president of the Swedish Red Cross. I've asked him to say a few words."

Folke said: "May I first express the gratitude of the Swedish Government and Swedish Red Cross for the privilege of taking part in this humanitarian work. . . . At this very moment the exchange of 4,159 British soldiers is taking place in this Swedish port; 831 German repatriables are being sent back to Germany by train and boat. It is our sincere hope that this type of exchange may be repeated in the future."

The next day, CBS News correspondent Bernhard Valery gave a similarly positive report: "We, the Allied correspondents who came to Gothenburg to follow the exchange, were afraid of meeting all these boys. We feared that physical and moral suffering has made them bitter and resentful. We discovered, however, that it takes more than a lost leg or arm to make an invalid out of a brave man. . . . The man whose authority and untiring energy was largely responsible for the success of the exchange operation . . . is by my side now . . . Count Bernadotte."

"These rather strenuous days have been some of the most happy days of my life," Folke told Valery. "From all sides, both American, British and German, I have received many times word of appreciation and thanks, and that of course makes me very happy. But when I will think back on the result of these days I know that I am the one who ought to be thankful. Thankful for having had the privilege to lead this operation and see how lights of happiness have come in the eyes of all these American, British and German repatriables . . . their happiness has been the best reward for my work."

At last, Count Bernadotte had found a way to put his well of unfocused energy and idealism to good use.

Folke's accomplishments as part of the Red Cross paved the way for a bright new career of substance. After years of trial and error, he had finally landed on his dream job. He wanted to follow in the footsteps of his uncle, Prince Carl, and become Sweden's leading humanitarian. And so no sooner was the triumphal exchange of POWs over than Folke was off on his foreign travels again. In November 1943, he proceeded to Switzerland to try to expand the capacity of future prisoner exchanges. His first course of action was to interest the German Red Cross and the Nazi authorities in the continued repatriation of medical personnel, invalid prisoners of war, and perhaps even civilians.

Folke and Prince Carl were particularly anxious to assist the very poorly treated Russian prisoners of war in Germany, provided that the same could be done for Germans in Russia. The Russians being held by Germany (as well as the Germans being held by Russia) were treated even more horribly than the rest of the POWs. Again, the sticking point was that — like the Japanese — the Russians had never ratified the Geneva Convention about the treatment of prisoners of war. Therefore, there was no international law to guarantee protection for Soviet soldiers. Worse, the Germans had always regarded Soviet prisoners of war not only as despised enemies but also as racially inferior. The Russians at Stalag 17-B were housed adjacent to the barracks where Howard Thornley and the other Americans lived. With starvation and disease costing nearly every Russian at the stalag his life within months, daily burial brigades outside the Soviet barracks were a familiar scene, Thornley recalled. More than a dozen bodies were brought out every morning. Then another group would be brought in, and the heinous cycle would begin again.

If the Red Cross had a tough time dealing with the unyielding Germans, the Soviets proved even more hard-nosed. Although the agency had repeatedly asked for permission to send material aid to prisoners of war in Russian camps, the Soviet government had simply ignored the appeals. Soviet officials hadn't even shared a list of prisoners of war in Russia, despite several requests. These issues were never going to go away without intensive preparatory work carried out by a leading Red Cross official. Since Carl was too frail to endure rigorous travel, especially in wartime conditions, Folke was given the opportunity to show off his judiciousness. Folke traveled to Switzerland to persuade the Swiss to agree to Swedish intervention. He spoke ad nauseam with

International Red Cross officials in Geneva, explaining why it was so important to establish an open a dialogue between the Soviets and the Swedish Red Cross. Much to Folke's surprise, the Swiss quickly agreed to have the Swedes intervene, and so a hopeful Folke flew on to Berlin to negotiate with the chiefs of the German Red Cross.

But his visit was ill-timed. It coincided with an aggressive new scheme by the Allies to smash Germany into submission by leveling its greatest city.

CHAPTER SIX

Utter Chaos

On November 22, 1943, Folke Bernadotte was in Berlin. Determined to find a way to work with the German Red Cross on an exchange of Russian and German prisoners of war, he went straight to the top: the agency's head, Ernst-Robert Grawitz. Rarely have two more different people sat at the opposite ends of a negotiating table.

Grawitz was a die-hard Nazi and a close follower of SS leader Heinrich Himmler. As a physician, he advised Himmler on the best way to make the most of gas chambers, and he was the ringleader of Nazi efforts to "eradicate the perverted world of the homosexual" and to find a "cure" for homosexuality — efforts that involved experimentation on inmates in the concentration camps. Grawitz also had been an integral part of the Nazi team assigned to identify and do away with mentally ill and physically handicapped people since the effort began in 1939. In the months following his meeting with Folke, as the end of the war drew to a close, Grawitz also would serve as a doctor to Hitler and his inner circle. When, in early 1945, word got out that most officials were fleeing Berlin in order to escape the advancing Soviet Army, Grawitz pleaded with Hitler that he be allowed to do the same. Absolutely not, Hitler said. And so, on April 24, Grawitz was eating dinner with his wife and children when he pulled the pins out of two grenades he was holding under the table and exterminated his entire family.

But when he met with Folke on November 22, 1943, Grawitz only talked about what a keen interest the German Red Cross took in the welfare of the country's concentration camp inmates. Wherever you looked, the setup was good, he claimed, with food, clothes, housing, and medical care all satisfactory. He even went so far as to postulate that the living standards in the camps were on par — or even better — than what most of the inmates were used to in their regular lives. His eyes widened in feigned sympathy, but the slight smile on his face said otherwise. All Grawitz really cared about was that any actions taken by the German Red Cross were in sync with Nazi policies. The agency had long ago lost its independence and, for all practical purposes, was now nothing but a mere lackey for Hitler. Despite Folke's best intentions, the discussions, in the end, went nowhere. But Folke should have expected this. An exchange of Russian and German POWs was always going to be a monumental task, nearly impossible to pull off.

Since the Russians had never ratified the Geneva Conventions, the International Committee of the Red Cross (ICRC) had never been able to establish even a back channel to communicate with Soviet authorities on the issue. Years earlier, the ICRC had stationed a permanent delegate in Moscow, but he was recalled in 1938, as there was nothing for him to do there. When Russia was drawn into the war, the agency emphasized the importance of collecting and forwarding information concerning wounded soldiers and prisoners. At first the Soviets seemed willing to comply, but that cooperation soon withered.

The Germans provided a preliminary list of Russian prisoners and similar lists were handed over by Finland and other countries; millions of names were forwarded to Moscow. But not a single tally could be extracted from the Russians. The ICRC even went so far as to say that Russians could handpick a group of six neutral delegates to travel to Russia to help with the task. Russia wasn't budging.

Nor did the ICRC make substantial inroads with Germany, with which it had a long and complicated history. From the time Hitler had been appointed chancellor in January 1933, cries for help for Jews began pouring into the agency. In April of that year, for instance, a Jewish refugee sent a letter to the ICRC describing the brutality at Dachau, the first concentration camp established by the Germans, which had opened a month earlier. "I beg you again in the name of the prisoners," he pleaded. "Help! Help!" Such appeals generated sympathy, but the ICRC's formal position was — again — tied to the Geneva Conventions, which protected soldiers but not civilians; the treatment and welfare of German Jews detained in camps in Germany was considered an internal matter. As Hitler's reprehensible intentions became clear, the ICRC did repeatedly try to extend an olive branch to the German Red Cross to see how the two might work together to help. But the German Red Cross was not an amenable partner; it had chosen to fall in lockstep with the regime rather than face the possibility of being shut down. Without its cooperation, the ICRC was working in a vacuum. Even Walther Georg Hartmann, head of the Foreign Section of the German Red Cross — often cited as one of the only real humanitarians in the leadership of the organization — had joined the Nazi Party in 1933 and was considered to be a loyal member. And so when Folke actually met with Hartmann, he did a delicate dance by merely hinting that the Germans might one day want to consider an exchange of prisoners.

Such were the types of obstacles and officials Folke found himself dealing with on November 22, 1943, when, as Folke put it, all hell broke loose. He was being hosted by the Swedish Legation and had been invited to dinner there that evening, after his meeting with Grawitz. No sooner had all parties exchanged pleasantries than a telephone call came in. An Allied attack on Berlin was imminent. He and the others weren't sure how seriously to take the warning, and so they nervously found their seats around the table at about 7:30 p.m. Then the air raid sirens went off — noisy, clear, and followed immediately by the roar of approaching planes. Folke and the others shot up out of their chairs, cleared the room, and raced to the shelter beneath the Legation that had just been completed by Swedish workmen.

"This was obviously a large-scale raid," Folke later wrote. "Fire wardens soon reported that incendiary bombs had set fire to the attic and we rushed to extinguish the blaze. However, it was too dangerous to fight the fire immediately because of the raid, and we returned to the shelter. More and more Swedes, who had first fled to cellars in the houses where they lived, soon arrived. These cellars were not strong enough to resist the concussion of explosions and falling masonry. We learned that the other three Legation buildings were also on fire and that they were heavily damaged. The all-clear signal was sounded after an hour and a half, and we went out. The houses nearby were ablaze, and the fire burned fiercely in the attic of the Legation. While efforts were being made to extinguish it, we tried to save a number of valuables in the upper two floors. After that, we started carrying the Legation archives down to the shelter, where we were soon confined again by another alarm. This raid only lasted a short time, however. When the second all-clear came we found that all phone connections had been cut off and access to water was very limited. We tried to get out and walk to the nearest police station in an effort to have fire engines sent to the Legation, which could still be saved. I shall never forget the sights we witnessed. It was blowing hard. Soot and ashes from burning houses were whirling about, and we were nearly blinded. Sirens screamed as fire engines rushed by. The streets were full of people, apathetic, worn, and tired. That night in Berlin was one of the most terrible I have ever experienced."

Despite all that chaos, Folke said he did not regret being there. Amid this mayhem, staring death in the face, he learned how insignificant a single person was in a global conflict. That fiery night in Berlin thoroughly impressed upon Folke the appalling realities of all-out war. He was in the thick of the action — and yet somehow it hadn't terrified him.

That night, the second major raid in the Battle of Berlin, hundreds of British and Canadian Lancasters, Stirlings, and Halifaxes rained more than 2,300 tons of bombs down on the city in the space of 30 minutes, destroying the former British Embassy, the landmark Kaiser Wilhelm Church, the Charlottenburg Palace, the department store KaDeWe, and much of the Berlin Zoo. Thanks to the dry weather, firestorms popped up everywhere, sending smoke columns 19,000 feet into the air. More than 2,000 Berliners died in the attack, and nearly 200,000 people were rendered homeless, many of whom crammed into makeshift shelters to wait out the continuing raids. The following night, another 1,000 were killed and another 100,000 were left with nowhere to live. It was the single most devastating air assault on Berlin of the entire war.

Joseph Goebbels, the Nazis' minister of propaganda, wrote in his diary: "I just can't understand how the English are able to do so much damage to the Reich capital in one air raid. The picture that greeted my eyes in Wilhelmsplatz [a large city square] was one of utter devastation ... . Blazing fires everywhere. . . . Hell itself seems to have broken loose over us."

The Allies had been confident that the destruction of Berlin would be the crushing blow that would break the German will once and for all. With a population of four million, the capital city was unequivocally the political and financial heart of the Third Reich. But it didn't happen quite that way. While no one could deny that the raids of

November 22 and 23 had a profound impact on Berliners, in the end, the bombing failed to sap the nation's morale. What helped keep spirits high was both the masterful job German authorities did when it came to firefighting and the prompt restoration of basic services. After the November raids, officials immediately rushed in 50,000 troops to clear away the rubble. And the government made its citizens feel safe and secure, as demonstrated by the resources allocated to air-raid shelters and warning systems.

But the bombing stayed with Folke for the rest of his life. "Total war had this night shown itself at its worst," he later wrote. "It nurtured bitter thoughts. So this was where civilization was leading us. Here was the drama which beset the life of modern man. The curtain had not only risen in Berlin, but also in London and Warsaw, Rotterdam and elsewhere. The whole thing was like a nightmare."

Folke remained passionate about his mission, but thanks to the indifference of authorities on both sides, the negotiation of a Russian-German exchange was becoming a mutating monster. Frustrated with the rash of obstacles, Folke switched gears, returning to Stockholm in late 1943 to pursue a different path. Historically, Sweden had enjoyed a close relationship with Poland, which won its independence in 1918. During 123 years of occupation, the Polish people had stubbornly fought to hold on to their history, culture, and language. Being sympathetic to their plight, Folke turned his attention to the millions of Poles who had been displaced by the dual invasions by Germany and the Soviet Union in September 1939 — Germany from the west and Russia from the east soon afterward. Along with Yugoslavia, Poland was the country that bore the biggest brunt of the war's devastation, especially since Nazi ideology viewed Poles as subhumans squatting on lands vital to Germany. Between 1939 and 1945, six million people, or more than 15 percent of Poland's population, perished. By the end of the war, another three million would be displaced.

Folke tried to connect with the Polish government-in-exile, formed in the aftermath of the 1939 invasion. That government had been based in Paris until 1940, when it was moved to London after France fell under German control. Despite military defeat, the Polish government itself never surrendered, and the Allies accepted the government-in-exile as the legitimate representative of the Polish people. Indeed, the Poles organized one of the largest underground movements in Europe in response to the German occupation, over which the exiled government exerted considerable influence. Folke knew that Britain would surely be grateful for anything that could be done for the Poles, since it had gone to war on their behalf, and had been unable to do little for them itself. If he accomplished anything, plenty of goodwill from the western powers would be his reward.

But, as was so often the case, Folke's plan was an overly ambitious one that would cost millions of dollars — if not a lot more — and possibly yield little results. He envisioned the creation of a huge camp somewhere inside Sweden, complete with homes, schools, and even recreational facilities, where displaced Poles could rebuild their physical and emotional strength before being returned to their home country. Folke hired architects to come up with a rendering of a design, making it seem as though the idea was actually plausible. The initiative even had the support of the Swedish government, which he had approached on the matter. The only condition the government imposed was that the Poles and other interested governments would have to be active participants in the scheme. Sweden wasn't going to go it alone.

So on the night of February 12, 1944, Folke traveled to Bromma Airport outside Stockholm to catch a plane that the British Legation had put at his disposal. He was to fly to London to meet the Polish government representatives, the British Red Cross, and the United Nations Relief and Rehabilitation Administration, which had been founded only three months earlier. By this time, there was no more regular air service between Sweden and England. However, the British Legation allowed him to hop a ride via one of the very fast and tiny Mosquito planes used for ferrying mail between Stockholm and London.

While Folke sat crammed into the narrow bomb bay, the pilot spoke to him like a schoolteacher, insisting he memorize every last detail about how a parachute works. "You had better sit tight," explained the pilot with a wink, "in case the bomb bay doors open. I should hate to lose you." Folke was given an oxygen mask as the twin-engine, shoulder-winged machine climbed to 25,000 feet over German-occupied Norway. Cold air wafted up through the crack in the bomb bay doors, through which Folke could sneak a peek at a starry night sky. After nearly four hours of turbulent flying, a very stiff Folke landed safely and disembarked at Leuchars, Scotland.

The next morning, he was off to London, a city he hadn't seen since attending the 1937 coronation of George VI with his family and parents-in-law. The war had brought out the best in King George VI, an inspiring figure who boosted British morale by visiting bombed areas and touring war zones. He also made a series of rousing radio broadcasts encouraging Britons to stand firm, for which he had to overcome a debilitating stutter. George and his wife, Elizabeth, enjoyed a rare solidarity with their subjects, especially when the two overruled requests from the government that they relocate to the safety of Canada. The day after a Luftwaffe bomb landed on Buckingham Palace, that solidarity became mutual. "I'm glad we've been bombed," Queen Elizabeth said memorably. "Now we can look the East End in the face."

Once there, Folke could more easily get a sense of the English population's reaction to air warfare and compare it with that of the Germans. The first thing he noted was that there was much less demolition in London than in Berlin and that the situation was not as dire as he'd been led to believe. It was true that London and many other English towns had endured frightful bombing attacks and suffered great losses. But by and large, German propaganda in that respect had been greatly exaggerated, and London looked pretty much the way he had remembered it. The Londoners he met showed unblinking fortitude in the face of adversity and had even managed to retain their trademark dry British sense of humor.

Folke met with Anthony Eden, Winston Churchill's foreign secretary, a polished and mannerly politician who enjoyed a great deal of public backing. Folke delivered a letter to Eden from Prince Carl, seeking the British government's cooperation in launching a new round of prisoner exchanges. This exchange, Prince Carl noted, should be more ambitious than the previous one so that it could include civilian internees. Eden promised to have his experts investigate the idea's feasibility and to report back via the Swedish minister. They also talked about how best to persuade Russia to collaborate in a POW exchange. On the whole, Eden seemed keenly interested in Folke's proposition. His gratitude for the prisoner of war exchanges that had taken place the previous fall in Gothenburg was palpable. Folke had become a man of stature, and this helped him gain access to the ears of the most influential people.

Folke had two other memorable encounters while in London. One was a meeting with King Haakon VII of Norway, a man Folke admired for his courage and unwavering stance against the German invaders. When the Nazis stormed into Norway in the spring of 1940, the king led the opposition, rallying his people to defy the enemy. He vowed to abdicate if he got even the slightest whiff that anyone in his government was cooperating with the attackers. After establishing a government-in-exile in London, King Haakon became the foremost symbol of the Norwegian people's resistance against a brutal occupation. His prolific radio broadcasts served as a source of inspiration. When he returned from exile in 1945, an enthusiastic throng of spectators lined the streets of Oslo to welcome him.

Folke's other big meeting was with the widowed Queen Maria of Yugoslavia. Like King Haakon, she and her family also were forced into exile in London, where she was very active from afar in organizing relief efforts for her people, who had suffered almost as much as the Poles. She asked Folke if the Swedish Red Cross could somehow get aid to the thousands of Yugoslavs that the Germans had relocated to Norway. She had heard they were living in deplorable conditions. Folke promised to do all he could, but when he took up the idea with German officials, they were quick to dismiss it. Folke wasn't surprised.

Before Folke left London, where he had at least managed to make some of the necessary contacts to help with his Polish scheme, he was asked to release a statement to the Swedish press. No matter how tentative, plans for another exchange of prisoners of war had to be kept secret from the public, as no one had any idea what the outcome would be. Even so, Folke decided to conduct a bold experiment. He would tell them the truth and trust reporters not to share it. Believing it better for the media to get information directly from him rather than through the rumor mill, he told them about the negotiations in Geneva and London that he hoped would lead to an exchange within a year. He asked that nothing be published about it, explaining that he didn't want to raise false hopes in the various prison camps. There could be no repeat of the disappointment experienced by so many soldiers earlier in the war. The Swedish press agreed to keep the news private and didn't publish a word. He later said that he had learned a good lesson: being frank with the press is better than lying.

The next several months were spent behind closed doors with various aid organizations in talks that led to no further movement on the POW exchange front. On the battlefield, however, the Allies were gaining lots of ground. From June 1944 to August 1944, the Allies took the fight straight to the Axis powers. Codenamed Operation

Overlord, the battle began on June 6, 1944, also known as D-Day, when an incredible armada of 156,000 American, British, and Canadian forces landed on five beaches along a 60-mile stretch of heavily fortified coastline in France's Normandy region, 24,000 by air and the rest by sea. The Normandy landings have been called the beginning of the end of war in Europe. The day before, on the morning of June 5, the Supreme Allied Commander General Dwight D. Eisenhower had given the go-ahead for the operation after his meteorologist predicted decent weather conditions. He told the troops: "You are about to embark upon the Great Crusade, toward which we have striven these many months. The eyes of the world are upon you."

In October 1944, Folke flew to liberated Paris, where he was to confer with Allied representatives regarding Sweden's role in post-war reconstruction. Because he had been in charge of the organization that oversaw the welfare of American airmen in Sweden, he had been invited to meet Eisenhower at the Allied headquarters at Versailles. General Curtis LeMay of the American Air Force, who had inspected the American fliers forced down in Sweden, briefed Eisenhower on Folke's background and first proposed a meeting.

Never showy or impulsive, Eisenhower was an honest, outgoing, and optimistic leader who had risen quickly through the ranks. After the United States entered the war in December 1941, Army Chief of Staff George Marshall had appointed him to the War Plans Division in Washington, where he prepared strategy for an Allied invasion of Europe. Promoted to major general in March 1942, and named head of the operations division of the War Department, Eisenhower advised Marshall to create a single post that would oversee all U.S. operations in Europe. Marshall did just that, and on June 11 stunned Eisenhower by awarding him the job after passing over 366 senior officers. On June 25, 1942, Eisenhower took command at U.S. headquarters in London. A few weeks later, he was named lieutenant general and picked to lead Operation Torch, the Allied invasion of French North Africa. As supreme commander of a mixed force of Allied nationals, Eisenhower was able to harmonize disparate personalities into a cohesive coalition. He was patient and calm in the face of uncertainty, winning the respect of his British and Canadian subordinates. From North Africa, he successfully directed the invasions of Tunisia, Sicily, and the Italian mainland, and in December 1943 was appointed Supreme Allied Commander of the Allied Expeditionary Force.

Folke couldn't have been more eager to meet him.

After landing on a temporary airstrip near Versailles, Folke got a close-up look at the Allies' destruction of the occupying forces in France and of the factories and transport networks that supported the German war effort. It was an awful sight. Some 400,000 buildings had been flattened, and five times that many were damaged. The French population also fared poorly. They were sick and very, very hungry. Two-thirds of children were suffering from rickets, while one child in ten did not survive childbirth. Food was so scarce that rationing remained in place even after the war until 1949.

Folke and Eisenhower were joined at their meeting by the American ambassador to Britain, John Winant, a talented diplomat whose own son, a first lieutenant in the U.S. Army, had been captured by the Germans in October 1943. John Winant Jr. became one of Himmler's personal hostages and wouldn't be freed until May 7, 1945. As such, Winant Sr. had a vested interest in Folke's work.

One of the main topics discussed by the three men was the gargantuan relief effort that would be required in Poland after the war. Eisenhower said he had no problem with the Swedish Red Cross contacting the Polish authorities directly to get a sense of the scope of such an undertaking, and encouraged Folke to do just that. Eisenhower repudiated the notion widely held by those in the United Nations Relief and Rehabilitation Administration that neutral assistance should not be accepted for post-war reconstruction work. He said: "All offered help should be made use of." He argued that as soon as an occupied country was liberated, it should be left to establish its own administration and thereafter be treated as a sovereign state with which neutral organizations could make contact and organize post-war work.

Talks between Folke and Eisenhower's team progressed at a nice clip — that is, until Hitler decided on a final, desperate gamble. In late 1944, more than 200,000 German troops and nearly 1,000 tanks launched the Nazi leader's last-ditch effort to turn the tide of war in Hitler's favor. Seeking to drive to the coast of the English Channel and split the Allied armies, the Germans mounted a blitzkrieg in the Ardennes Forest, a 75-mile stretch of dense woods and few roads. This climactic counteroffensive in Belgium, dubbed the Battle of the Bulge, forced Eisenhower to abandon Folke's relief discussions. But before he left, Eisenhower shared his plans for victory in Europe with Folke, who couldn't help but make a mental note of the absence of any details on how to save prisoners in German camps.

Folke said this about Eisenhower: "The Supreme Commander made a very strong impression on me. I realized that in him I was meeting a man of really big dimensions, as forceful as he was warm-hearted and generous by nature. He appeared reposed and calm, absolutely certain of reaching his goal and carrying out the gigantic task which had been imposed upon him. Here was obviously a man who knew what he wanted and had at his disposal the means of getting it. But what stood out above everything else about him was his humor. It gleamed through in practically everything which he said and gave a very human stamp to his whole personality. He gave no impression of harboring any hate against those who were his enemies in this Second World War — anyway not against the military leaders in the enemy camp — and in contrast to his underlings he was absolutely free from unbending militarism. This last attribute probably does more to explain, as far as I can make out, his supreme quality: his magnificent capacity for holding the western allies' leading representatives together."

Shortly after meeting Eisenhower, Folke attended what would turn out to be a fortuitous lunch at the Hotel Bristol. There, he was surrounded by the best and brightest members of the Swedish government and Swedish Red Cross, including the highly respected Raoul Nordling, the Swedish consul who had remained in Paris throughout the Nazi occupation. Nordling — described by Folke as "fearless" — had acted as a key mediator between the German occupation authorities and the Allied powers and the French patriotic forces, and had used his diplomatic immunity to prevent countless people from being deported to concentration camps. His efforts also led to the evacuation of foreign diplomats from Warsaw during the German invasion. Nordling encouraged Folke to find a way to provide assistance for French internees in Germany, especially the 20,000 French women barely holding on amid the horrific conditions at the Ravensbrück concentration camp.

Nordling's enthusiasm was infectious, and Folke was inspired by his dedication to rescuing others. "What especially interested and thrilled me was his account of how he had been able to prevent large numbers of women and men from being deported to Germany," he later wrote. "And how he had succeeded in persuading the Germans to release a number of Frenchmen who had been imprisoned in France at the time of the capitulation of Paris. Nordling is not a civil servant who fears responsibility and takes cover under regulations and instructions but fearlessly acts on his own responsibility. Without these qualities, he could never have succeeded in his self-imposed mission. As I listened to him, I became infected by his enthusiasm," Folke said. "I asked myself if I couldn't do something similar for those who were languishing in German concentration camps. Thus, a seed was sown in me."

That seed was cultivated further after Folke returned to Stockholm in December 1944 to meet with his personal friend, the Norwegian diplomat, Niels Christian Ditleff, a career diplomat and man who had also thrown himself heavily into humanitarian work. By the end of 1944, there were many thousands of Scandinavian prisoners in German concentration camps, including approximately 8,000 Norwegians and 6,000 Danes. The majority of these prisoners were not Jewish, and had been arrested for a variety of so-called offenses. When Folke broached the subject of the fate of these prisoners, Ditleff responded, "If any positive result is to be reached and carried through it is necessary to try and get into contact with the SS chief, minister of the interior and Reichsminister, Heinrich Himmler." Folke recalled Himmler's early speeches in which he had expressed an affinity for the northern countries and their people. There was a slight chance, Folke decided then and there, that Ditleff may be on to something.

Folke hadn't yet been able to accomplish an exchange between Russian and German prisoners of war — a serious disappointment, considering that out of 5.7 million Soviet soldiers captured between 1941 and 1945, more than 3.5 million would die in captivity. But he began to wonder whether the Swedish Red Cross might be able to assist and even rescue prisoners in concentration camps. It would be quite the accomplishment: the Germans had consistently refused to allow foreign observers to make even the most superficial investigations into the camps, and the Geneva Conventions didn't cover political prisoners there.

Folke was fairly certain he couldn't rely on any help from the western powers. In August 1944, they had refused pleas from Jewish organizations to bomb the extermination camps at Auschwitz or even the railway lines leading to the gas chambers. British and American media reports focused only minimally on the concentration camps and the ongoing murders; the fates of German-held Allied war prisoners commanded immeasurably greater interest than that of the Jews. Cries for action failed, for the most part, to get the attention of anyone who could have made a difference.

The full weight of the western Allies' endgame was instead applied to one job and one job only: decimating the German war machine. Nor were separate negotiations with Nazi Germany contemplated — not even if concentration camp prisoners could be saved. The goal was quite simple: Germany's unconditional surrender, after which the prisoners could be considered. Moreover, the United States and Britain were caught up in an equally high-stakes game against Japan, and for the Americans the fight in the Pacific was the most important scene of battle due to the Japanese bombing of Pearl Harbor in 1941.

But as Sweden searched for a broader role for itself and additional ways to improve its reputation as a neutral country, Folke's name was mentioned more and more at the most important government meetings. Apart from Sweden's genuine humanitarian bent, Stockholm was eager to create a better image for itself in order to survive and even thrive in an Anglo-American-dominated future. Were the conditions now ripe for a large-scale rescue of the people of all races, religions, and nationalities languishing in camps?

CHAPTER SEVEN

A Deal with the Devil

When Leo Goldberger, a retired New York University researcher now living in Massachusetts, was only 13, he got the scare of his life. It was 1943, and he was living in German-occupied Denmark when his family heard rumors of an impending mass deportation of Jews. Sure enough, one night in August, the Gestapo showed up at his family's apartment to fetch Goldberger's father, a cantor at a large Copenhagen synagogue.

"My dad came into my bedroom and told me to be quiet. He was not going to open the door," Goldberger told the *Washington Post* in 2016. "I remember pleading with him to open the door because I was afraid they would break in and shoot everyone."

But eventually the officers left. The next morning, he and his father learned that 12 prominent Danish Jews had been carted off, along with about seven dozen other Danes. If Goldberger's father had opened the door, he might have been among them.

Nazi Germany had occupied Denmark in April 1940. After years of relative calm, during which the Danes retained their own government, the Germans were cracking down. In September 1943 — just before the start of the Jewish new year — Denmark's 7,800 or so Jews were tipped off by a German diplomat that the Nazis planned to deport them all to concentration camps. As the news spread, most·everyone scrambled to hide themselves.

For the Nazis, the mission was supposed to be a breeze. Armed with a list of addresses, small teams — each made up of SS men and one Danish guide — planned to fan out across Copenhagen and round up the Jews, who would be at home observing Rosh Hashanah. Every Jew they could get their hands on would be sent to a Nazi extermination camp. But, for the most part, the houses and apartments they called on were empty. The Jews had gone elsewhere, thanks to an outpouring of compassion from ordinary Danes, who took them in. But the Goldbergers and the others might not have been able to flee anywhere outside of Denmark if not for the efforts of Niels Bohr, the famous Danish physicist.

While the Jews were fighting for their lives in the fall of 1943, Bohr — whose mother was Jewish — was being spirited to the United States via Sweden to work on the Manhattan Project. Although the United States had asked Sweden to get him out of the country immediately — so that he could get to work as fast as possible in America — Bohr refused to go anywhere until after he had the chance to meet with King Gustaf V. His wish was granted. Bohr demanded that the country guarantee asylum to all of Denmark's Jews. Only then would he agree to leave. It's not clear how much impact Bohr's demand had, but on October 2, a declaration was broadcast over Swedish radio: If Danish Jews could make it to Sweden, the country would take them in. Jews beat a hasty retreat out of Copenhagen whether by car, train, or foot. Within a two-week period, fishermen helped ferry 7,220 Danish Jews and 680 non-Jewish family members to safety across the narrow body of water separating Denmark from Sweden — including the Goldbergers. Unfortunately, 482 Jews didn't make it and were sent to the Theresienstadt concentration camp in Czechoslovakia.

While Denmark is often praised for being the only Nazi-occupied country to rescue nearly all its Jews, the question of whether Sweden could have done more during the war has been the subject of exhaustive debate over many decades. In the early years, Sweden's supposed neutrality in fact leaned in Germany's favor. Economic interests — and geography — helped cement it. In April 1940, after the Nazis invaded Denmark and Norway, Sweden found itself penned in by Germans. And Germany's control of the Baltic Sea kept Sweden under a virtual blockade, no longer able to conduct substantive business with any foreign nation other than Germany. Before the war, 24 percent of Sweden's exports went to Britain and 18 percent went to Germany. After trade with Britain became impossible, nearly all of the goods formerly destined for Britain went to Germany instead. The Swedes had little choice but to play nice. They needed German coal, and the Germans needed Sweden's high-grade iron ore (30 percent of that used by the German armaments industry), as well as ball bearings, foodstuffs, wood, and many other raw materials. In addition, Sweden imported oil and gasoline, chemicals, and rubber from Germany. The Swedes told themselves that cooperation with Germany was the only way to maintain their sovereignty.

Eventually, though, Sweden changed the way it saw the world. Heeding Allied warnings about neutrals doing business with Germany, Sweden slowly began extricating the country from the German economic and political web while shifting its allegiances toward the Allies. In May 1943, Sweden reopened trade relations with the western powers. Two months after that, the Swedish government announced that it would no longer permit Germany to transfer soldiers or war materials across its country.

As Sweden struggled for self-preservation, the Jewish part of the war equation was not a priority for over-whelmed Swedish decision-makers — at least not initially. Before the war, there were 7,000 Jews in Sweden, most of them living in Stockholm. In the early 1930s, about 3,000 Jews fled mainland Europe to Sweden because of its neu-trality. However, after the outbreak of war in the late 1930s, Sweden passed critical restrictions on immigration, as did many other countries at the time, which severely limited the number of Jews who could seek asylum there. In 1942, as news of the systematic persecution of Jews seeped out, Swedish diplomats sought to engage German authorities in negotiations to save Scandinavian Jews from deporta-tion, partly because fortunes had turned in the Allies' favor but also because Jewish organizations in Stockholm had put more pressure on Swedish authorities. The first major move to accept Jewish refugees occurred in November 1942, when Norwegian Jews faced deportation. Justifiably alarmed, the Swedish public made their concerns known, which prodded the government to take action, providing refuge for nearly half of Norway's Jews who managed to escape across the Norwegian-Swedish border. Then, in the fall of 1943, Sweden opened its doors to Danish Jews. Another huge effort to help occurred in 1944, when Raoul Wallenberg, a Swedish businessman, rescued thousands of Hungarian Jews in Budapest by issuing Swedish protective passes and moving them into houses under Swedish protection. Unfortunately, he was arrested by Soviet officials in January 1945 and never seen again.

Despite these initial steps to rescue the Jews, by the end of 1944 there were at least a million prisoners still being held in Nazi camps. No matter how cornered he may have become, Hitler's morbid mind never stopped mulling the "Jewish issue." Jesus most certainly was not a Jew, he insisted to his private secretary, Martin Bormann, on November 30, 1944. "The Jews would never have delivered one of their own to the Romans and to a Roman court; they would have convicted him themselves. It seems that many descendants of Roman legionnaires lived in Galilee and Jesus was one of them. It could be that his mother was Jewish." He continued to hammer away at his favorite themes: the Jews' obsession with money, the link between Jews and communism, the idea that all Jews should be murdered.

And no effort was spared to pursue his obsession. That year, so late in the war, Klaus Barbie, chief of the Nazi Gestapo in Lyons during the German occupation of France, led a raid of a home for Jewish children in Izieu, a remote hilltop village. He relayed the details to Heinz Röthke, a

German attorney, in a telex: "This morning the Jewish children's home 'Colonie d'Enfants' in Izieu, Ain was cleaned out. . . . Neither cash nor other valuables could be secured. Transport to Drancy to follow on 4/7/44." On that early April morning, as the children and their counselors were eating breakfast, Barbie and his men rounded up 45 youngsters (the one non-Jewish child was subsequently released to his cousin in town) and seven adults, loading them onto waiting trucks that took them to the concentration camp in Drancy, France, and then on to Auschwitz. Not one of them survived. For Barbie, it was just one more successful catch.

But Allied chiefs in London and Washington had little interest in rescuing Jews as they pursued their military objectives; again, they believed the only way to truly help inmates was to secure a total victory. Yet that victory was still months away, and reports of atrocities were mounting.

The International Committee of the Red Cross had long seemed paralyzed when it came to the Holocaust. In December 1939, the ICRC president had approached the German Red Cross to arrange for his delegates to visit Jews who had been deported to Poland. The request was met with a stern no. Under no circumstances did German authorities want outsiders visiting the camps. From then on, the ICRC addressed the question of Jews only indirectly, in generalities concerning the victims of mass arrests or deportation and without reference to their religious affiliation or racial origin. On April 29, 1942, the German Red Cross informed the ICRC that it would not communicate any information on "non-Aryan" detainees, and requested it stop asking questions. In the summer of 1942, The ICRC debated whether to launch a general appeal on violations of international humanitarian law. It prepared a draft, but decided in the end not to go forth with the matter, believing it would be a waste of time.

With the ICRC mostly impotent, pleas for help were increasingly lobbed at Folke and his more nimble and effective Swedish Red Cross. As the Allied fronts penetrated deeper into Germany, the start of 1945 was viewed as a race against time and a matter of life and death for the Jews still in captivity. No matter how the war played out, it would be potentially catastrophic for the prisoners. The Nazis planned to blow up camps and execute all remaining prisoners before the Allied forces had a chance to reach their objectives. Discussions of a rescue expedition had been going on for a while in Sweden, but no concrete plans had yet been made.

To most Allied observers, anyone considering a mass prisoner rescue was delusional. Even stepping foot inside the war zone was risky business. Intelligence about the location of camps and who was imprisoned there was limited, and Hitler had made it very clear that he would never grant prisoner releases — especially of Jews. But Sweden had its own reasons to mount a rescue operation. By 1944, with an Allied victory just over the horizon, even the pretense of neutrality had become an untenable position to be in. Any rescue operation offered the country the chance to atone for its sins in the final days of war. The Swedes also were in an enviable situation; they had unusually accurate information about what was actually occurring in the camps, and good cause to believe that prisoners might be released — not by Hitler but on the authority of Heinrich Himmler, who ran the camps. Though it was Hitler's intent to fight on until the very last minute, by the end of 1944, Himmler's aides were quietly disseminating word that the SS chief had accepted that the end was near and so was looking for an escape route. Intermediaries said Himmler would avail himself of any opportunity to talk peace with the Allies. He would also free prisoners as bait to lure the Allies to the table. The problem was that London and Washington had "no truck with Himmler," as Churchill put it. The Swedes, on the other hand, saw no reason not to take advantage of the overtures.

Folke conferred with his uncle, Prince Carl, chairman of the Swedish Red Cross, as well as with the Swedish government. It was agreed that it made more sense for a private individual than for a government minister to attempt to make fresh contact with the Nazis. A diplomat would be hamstrung, bound to make his approach through the Foreign Office, the head of which, Foreign Minister Joachim von Ribbentrop, was known to be at loggerheads with the Gestapo chief. Seasoned Swedish officials weren't sure the one-time head of the Swedish Boy Scouts would be up to the challenge, but others thought Himmler would find Folke's royal blood and sophisticated air alluring. Folke eagerly embraced the almost impossible task at hand.

And so by the beginning of February 1945, Folke had obtained his government's permission to try and make a direct personal approach to Himmler.

Folke had an excellent ready-made excuse to visit Berlin at that time, because the Swedish Red Cross had just sent a delegation there to try to retrieve Swedish-born women who had married Germans but who were now widowed or deserted. Ostensibly in order to meet up with this delegation, Folke flew to Tempelhof Airfield in Berlin on February 16, 1945. His actual purpose, however, was to see Himmler about all the imprisoned Scandinavians, and even inmates of other nationalities.

The 16th was none too soon. Although the Wehrmacht was finally crumbling, terrible violence raged on. On February 8, 1945, men from the Norwegian resistance group Milorg assassinated Karl Marthinsen, who played a key role in implementing the Holocaust in Norway. The Nazis retaliated by executing 29 Norwegians by firing squad. A terrible blitz rained down on Berlin on February 4 that led Joseph Goebbels, Hitler's minister for enlightenment and propaganda, to declare the capital "closed." A few weeks earlier, the Soviets had launched an offensive on January 12, liberating western Poland and forcing Hungary to surrender. On February 8, the Russians traveled across the River Oder and were a mere 33 miles from Berlin. From the 13th to the 15th, the Allies bombed the German city of Dresden, killing approximately 35,000 civilians. On February 12, the Yalta Conference brought together Winston Churchill, Joseph Stalin, and Franklin D. Roosevelt for a second time, with the organizing of the occupation of Germany a top priority. During the conference, the three leaders agreed to unify their military effort — especially in the Pacific — while planning for a postwar world.

From the start, Folke proposed to tackle his objective one step at a time. As he told his friend Major Sven Frykman: "It would be futile to ask the Germans to open their concentration camps and allow us to take their inmates away immediately. We must proceed by stages. First, we must get the Scandinavians assembled in one place in Germany near the Danish frontier so that we can keep an eye on them in case of a breakdown of the Nazi regime and . . . succor the sick and try and reduce the liquidations. The next step must be to get the Scandinavians over the border into Denmark and eventually to Sweden. Having inserted the thin end of the wedge, we must then try and get hold of specialized classes of non-Scandinavian prisoners, such as relatives of prominent Swedes, intellectuals and children. In the process we must lay our hands on anybody else we can and . . . by showing our faces, shame the Gestapo into mitigating some of the horrors of the camps. Finally we must make a general offensive against any concentration camps we can reach and enlist the collaboration of other neutral powers, such as the Swiss. This will not be achieved by table-thumping — only by firmness, tact and perseverance. We must use bribery — cigarettes, drink, chocolate or any other means we can think of — in order to achieve our purpose. We must not talk politics or get into any quarrels with the Germans. We must even, if necessary, flatter and cajole them — however much it may stick in our throats."

But first things first. Folke had to meet Himmler, who was just about the only person who still held some sway over Hitler.

Although still very loyal to Hitler, Himmler was smart enough to know that Germany wasn't going to win the war. Himmler knew he would need to save himself by playing a double game, exacting maximum brutality as Hitler would have it while quietly approaching the western powers. The

Allies showed no interest in his tentative gestures, however, so to illustrate his goodwill Himmler orchestrated the release of the five so-called "Warsaw Swedes," businessmen who had been sentenced to life in prison for espionage in 1943. Then, in the winter of 1944 and 1945, Himmler worked with Jean-Marie Musy, the former president of Switzerland, to barter the lives of Jews held in Theresienstadt for a ransom of 20 million Swiss francs from Jewish sources in the United States.

Then, in the winter of 1944 and 1945, Himmler worked with his old acquaintance, Jean-Marie Musy, former president of the Swiss Confederation, to take advantage of a narrow window of opportunity to curry international favor. Through high-level negotiations, Musy — along with his son Benoit Musy and German Foreign Intelligence Chief Walter Schellenberg — was able to facilitate the transfer of 1,200 prisoners from the Theresienstadt concentration camp to Switzerland in January 1945. Another 1,200 prisoners were to follow two weeks later, followed by another release two weeks after that. A "ransom" of about $1.25 million was placed in Swiss bank accounts by Jewish organizations active in Switzerland. But the deal went awry and the money was never paid to the Nazis. Himmler rescinded the directive and put a lid on the operation after an underling of his, Ernst Kaltenbrunner, chief of the Nazi Secret Police, revealed the plans to Hitler. After learning of Himmler's intentions, Hitler was enraged, shouting out orders that anyone caught exchanging prisoners be executed immediately. He summoned Himmler to his office and told him what he thought of his actions in terms that would be

Painting of General Bernadotte by François Gérard, 1812.

Count Bernadotte's father, Prince Oscar (left), with his brothers (left to right), Prince Carl, Prince Eugene, and King Gustaf V.

TOP: Folke Bernadotte at 18 months in 1896, holding a riding crop.

MIDDLE: Two-year-old Folke Bernadotte, first on the left, with his four older siblings: Elsa, Sophia, Carl, and Maria.

BOTTOM: With his brothers and sisters (left to right), Sophia, Elsa, Carl, Folke, Maria.

On parade with the Royal Life Guard Dragoons.

With his unit of Dragoons, Count Bernadotte is second row, center.

ABOVE: Actress Lillie Christina Ericson on stage.

RIGHT: Count Bernadotte and Lillie Ericson had a daughter, right, Jeanne Birgitta Sofia Kristina Ericson, together in 1921.

Folke and Estelle Bernadotte leaving the church after their marriage in Pleasantville, NY, 1928, while the Royal Life Guard Dragoons form the guard of honor.

As director of the exchange of disabled German, British, and American war prisoners, Count Bernadotte is examining identity documents at Göteborg Central Station in October, 1943.

Swedish Red Cross buses drive through Odense carrying Danish prisoners from German concentration camps as part of the White Buses operaton, April 17, 1945.

American troops
view inmates'
bodies at
Neuengamme.

The view of Neuengamme from above after liberation in 1945.

Women doing manual labor outside at Ravensbrück.

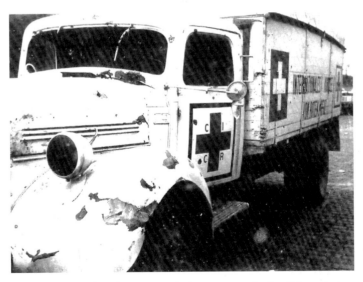

An International Red Cross truck that was attacked at Schwerin by the RAF on April 25, 1945. Two drivers, a Swede and a Canadian, and several women rescued from Ravensbrück concentration camp were killed in the attack.

Count Bernadotte speaks with German prisoners of war.

He takes shelter during an air raid.

Obergruppenführer
Ernst Kaltenbrunner.

Reichsführer Heinrich Himmler.

Brigadeführer Walter Schellenberg.

ABOVE: Count
Bernadotte receiving
a scroll from
Stockholm Rabbi
Wolf Jacobsson for
saving 10,000 Jews.

RIGHT: Count
Bernadotte with
German refugee
children in
June 1945.

Count Bernadotte with German refugee children in Berlin.

His Red Cross car at Schönhausen, Germany.

Count Folke Bernadotte on his 50th birthday in his Royal Life Guard Dragoons uniform, 1945.

Count Bernadotte rejoins his wife and their son on returning from a trip to Germany.

Count Bernadotte sailing with Scouts and Guides to the French Jamboree, 1947.

Count Bernadotte with 12-year-old son Bertil at home in Stockholm, 1947.

Count Bernadotte on the beach at Rhodes with his family in July 1948.

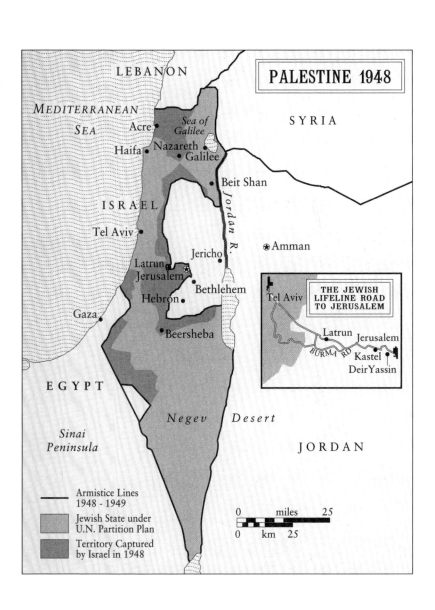

PALESTINE 1948

MEDITERRANEAN
SEA

LEBANON

SYRIA

Acre

Sea of
Galilee

Haifa

Nazareth

Galilee

Beit Shan

ISRAEL

Jordan R.

Tel Aviv

⁕Amman

Jericho

Latrun
Jerusalem

Bethlehem

Hebron

Gaza

Beersheba

EGYPT

Negev   Desert

JORDAN

Sinai
Peninsula

THE JEWISH
LIFELINE ROAD
TO JERUSALEM

Tel Aviv

Latrun

Jerusalem

BURMA RD.

Kastel

Deir Yassin

Armistice Lines
1948 - 1949

Jewish State under
U.N. Partition Plan

Territory Captured
by Israel in 1948

0   miles   25

0   km   25

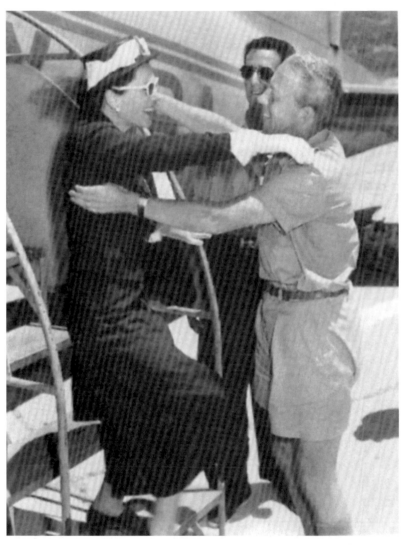

Count Bernadotte greets his wife, Estelle, when she arrives in Rhodes at his UN mediation headquarters.

Count Bernadotte confers with Moshe Sharett, future Israeli Foreign Minister.

Count Bernadotte with Moshe Sharett in Tel Aviv, September 1948.
(COURTESY OF GPO)

Count Bernadotte and Henrik Beer, General Secretary of the Swedish
Red Cross.

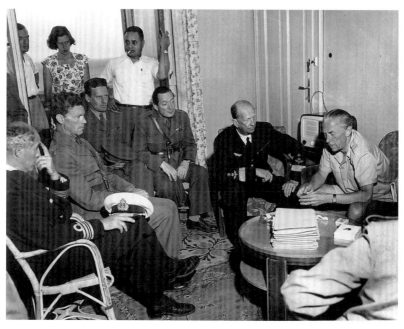

Count Bernadotte discussing the Palestine truce with the Swedish mission on
August 3, 1948. Count Bernadotte is far right, General Age Lundström is
next to him.

Count Bernadotte announces the Palestine Armistice from Shepherd Hotel, Cairo, on June 11, 1948.

Count Bernadotte and Barbro Wessel, secretary, working at his headquarters in Rhodes.

Count Bernadotte in front of his white United Nations plane with Paul Mohne (from left), Ralph Bunche, and (wearing a fez) the Lebanese Chief of protocol.

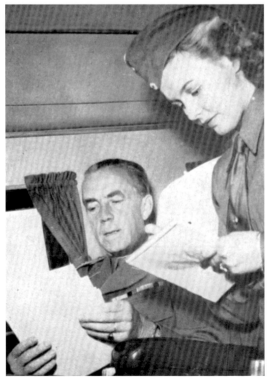

Count Bernadotte dictating to his Swedish Red Cross secretary aboard a plane.

Demonstration against Count Bernadotte by Lehi members, 1948.

Armed and vigilant Lehi members guard one of their Jerusalem camps, 1948.

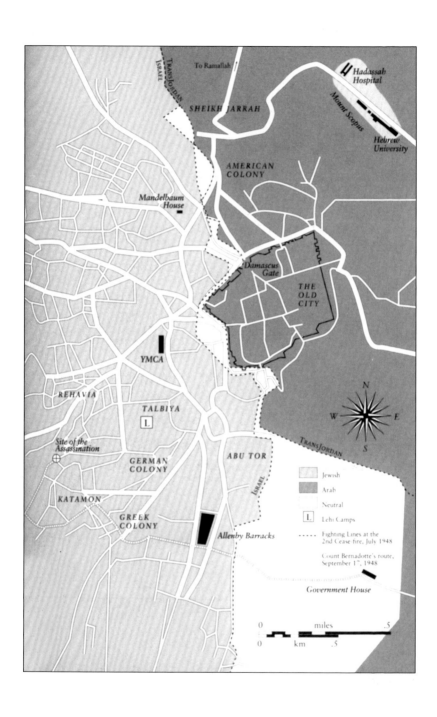

To Ramallah

SHEIKH JARRAH

Hadassah
Hospital

Mount Scopus

Hebrew
University

AMERICAN
COLONY

Mandelbaum
House

Damascus
Gate

THE
OLD
CITY

YMCA

REHAVIA

TALBIYA L

Site of the
Assassination

GERMAN
COLONY

ABU TOR

KATAMON

GREEK
COLONY

Allenby Barracks

TRANSJORDAN
ISRAEL

TransJordan

N
W   E
S

TransJordan

Israel

Jewish

Arab

Neutral

L   Lehi Camps

······ Fighting Lines at the
2nd Cease-fire, July 1948

Count Bernadotte's route,
September 17, 1948

Government House

0   miles   .5

0   km   .5

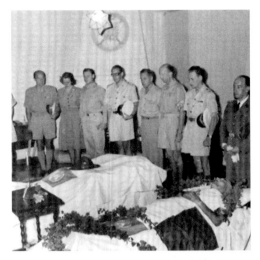

LEFT: Count Bernadotte and Colonel André Sérot lie in state in the Jerusalem YMCA on September 18, 1948.

RIGHT: The Security Council, in a special session in Paris, rise to mark the assassination of Count Folke Bernadotte with a moment of silence, September 18, 1948.

ABOVE: Nathan Yellin-Mor (wearing glasses) and Matityahu Shmuelevitz, Lehi leaders sentenced and then immediately amnestied in Israeli military court, 1948.

Official portrait of Lehi commander Yitzhak Shamir, who later became prime minister of Israel. Shown behind is a portrait of Avraham Stern, founder of Lehi.

David Ben-Gurion and Yehoshua Cohen in Ein Avdat, Israel. Cohen was Ben-Gurion's bodyguard and Count Bernadotte's assassin. Photo taken by Moshe Friedan. (COURTESY OF GPO)

Count Bernadotte lies in State at the Jerusalem YMCA, 1948.

Boy Scouts, Swedish, United Nations, and Red Cross banners march in the cortège.

ABOVE: The funeral
procession through
Stockholm. The coffin is
shrouded and decorated
with white carnations.

RIGHT: Bust of Count
Bernadotte in Stockholm.

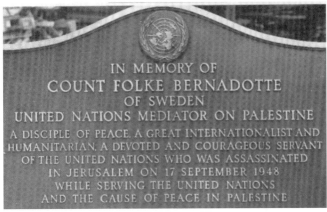

IN MEMORY OF
COUNT FOLKE BERNADOTTE
OF SWEDEN
UNITED NATIONS MEDIATOR ON PALESTINE
A DISCIPLE OF PEACE, A GREAT INTERNATIONALIST AND
HUMANITARIAN, A DEVOTED AND COURAGEOUS SERVANT
OF THE UNITED NATIONS WHO WAS ASSASSINATED
IN JERUSALEM ON 17 SEPTEMBER 1948
WHILE SERVING THE UNITED NATIONS
AND THE CAUSE OF PEACE IN PALESTINE

Memorial service at Gustav Vasa Church, Stockholm, September 26, 1948.

impossible to forget. "No camp inmate in the southern half of Germany must fall into enemy hands," he told Himmler. In other words, everyone must die.

Oddly enough, Folke and Himmler actually had quite a bit in common. Both, in spite of enjoying the outdoors and exercise, suffered from constant stomach issues. Both, while diligent, were never brilliant students. Both attended church and were fairly prim and proper as young men. Both enjoyed helping people, with Himmler often visiting the sick and assisting old people as a young man. The men even married in the same year, 1928, while harboring military career aspirations.

And yet Himmler went on to become Hitler's number two and the architect of the Holocaust, a man who fit mass murder and occasional visits to his mistress, Bunny, in between curling matches, sauna sessions, and phone calls to his family.

Although many of Himmler's diary pages were discovered shortly after the war, some 1,000 pages that had been missing for more than 70 years were discovered in 2016 in an archive in Moscow, where they were stashed in a folder labeled only with the word "diary." The diaries were published by Germany's *Bild* newspaper, with many of the details translated in the British press. The documents are being studied by the director of the German Historical Institute in Moscow, Nikolaus Katzen, who told *Bild* they are of "outstanding historical significance" and made him "shudder."

In them, Himmler noted everything from the banal details about his various working trips and leisure activities to his thoughts on the gassing of hundreds of prisoners and a lavish SS banquet he attended immediately after observing one such execution. In one entry, Himmler referred to a "comradely" lunch at the Dachau concentration camp, the scene of 41,500 murders. In another, he "took a snack in the café at the SS casino" at Buchenwald, where 56,000 people were killed. Himmler wrote of playing cards, gazing at the stars, or watching films in between meetings with Hitler and senior Nazi officials, during which they plotted and hashed over details of the Endlösung.

The paper reported that Himmler often began his days with two-hour massage sessions, and called home to speak with his wife, Margarete, and blond pigtailed daughter, Gudrun Burwitz — whom he called "Puppi" or little doll — nearly every day. (That ever-loyal daughter, who referred to her beloved father as "Papi," remained an unrepentant neo-Nazi until her death on May 24, 2018 at the age of 88.) One entry outlined how, one day in 1944, Himmler had a massage before overseeing the shooting of 10 Polish detainees. On the same day, he called for new guard dogs at Auschwitz "capable of ripping apart everyone but their handlers."

The diaries illustrate how Himmler was obsessed with astrology. He was absolutely captivated by the Aryan myths on which Nazi propaganda was built. He was also fascinated by strange diets and, in 1943, told Hitler that the trapped SS soldiers in Stalingrad should be fed the same dried rations as the ones that Genghis Khan gave his warriors.

"The most interesting thing for me is this combination of doting father and cold-blooded killer," Damian Imöhl, the journalist who helped track down the diaries for *Bild*, told the *Times of London*. "He was very careful about his wife and daughter, as well as his affair with his secretary. He takes care of his comrades and friends. Then there is the man of horror." One of the most notorious moments of the entire war was listed simply as "17:30 speech to SS officers." It referred to a talk Himmler made in Posen in which he addressed the "small matter" of the "extermination of the Jewish people."

On February 16, 1945, Folke arrived in Berlin. The day after, he was thrown directly into the heart of the Nazi jungle, meeting with none other than Kaltenbrunner, number two to Himmler in the Gestapo — the same Kaltenbrunner who had told Hitler about Himmler's attempted deal with Switzerland. No one looked the part quite like he did. With his scarred left cheek, the intense, steely-eyed Nazi appeared almost as a caricature of someone positioned high within the feared SS. And his record went hand in hand with his appearance. He directly controlled the killings in the concentration camps. After an attack on Hitler's life on July 20, 1944 — one of at least 15 separate attempts to murder Hitler — Kaltenbrunner's prestige and influence within the Nazi leadership only grew. And so by early 1945, Kaltenbrunner was a fixture of the diminishing inner circle around the increasingly deranged Hitler. As Folke said: "Obergruppenführer Kaltenbrunner was manifestly not a man who could conceive the slightest noteworthy understanding for humanitarian action in German concentration camps."

Folke met Kaltenbrunner at his luxurious villa in Wannsee, where he played the consummate host, offering a glass of Dubonnet and Chesterfield cigarettes as if they were old school chums enjoying a reunion. Folke described his demeanor as "polite, coolish and inquisitive." Kaltenbrunner was curious to know why Folke had come all that way to see his boss, Himmler. Folke explained that his only intention was to help the Scandinavian prisoners, and that's why he wanted Kaltenbrunner to arrange a meeting. He reminded Kaltenbrunner that Swedish-German relations were at an all-time low, in large part due to Germany's ruthlessness in Norway and Denmark. He also reminded Kaltenbrunner that Himmler had expressed a desire to bolster these deteriorating ties. Kaltenbrunner asked if Folke spoke for the Swedish government, to which Folke replied, "No. But not only the Swedish government but the whole Swedish people are behind me."

Brigadeführer Walter Schellenberg joined them. He was head of the German Foreign Intelligence, responsible for unmasking all internal plots against the Nazi regime. Although nominally subordinate to Kaltenbrunner, he was actually on friendlier terms with Himmler. (Later on, Folke had this to say about Schellenberg: "From the start I conceived a certain trust in him and, in any case, I shall always be grateful to him for the positive assistance he rendered me in connection with Red Cross work in Germany.")

The conversation continued, and Kaltenbrunner asked if Folke had any concrete proposal to put forth to Himmler. Folke said he was simply there to ascertain a guarantee of exit visas for those Swedes married to Germans. He did not want to reveal his real intention: to get Himmler's permission to rescue all Scandinavians — and hopefully others — from the concentration camps. Folke figured Kaltenbrunner "would naturally do everything to prevent my meeting Himmler" and so assumed honesty was definitely not the best policy. Surprisingly, Kaltenbrunner said he understood the importance of Folke seeing Himmler about the visas. The meeting ended with Folke not sure if he had succeeded or failed.

Next, Folke met Foreign Minister Joachim von Ribbentrop, who saw him for the same reason as Kaltenbrunner — to satisfy his rabid curiosity as to what business the Swede might have with the Gestapo chief.

Ribbentrop launched into a marathon speech lasting one hour and seven minutes about the state of politics — Folke timed it — without the Swede getting a single word in edgewise. The foreign minister covered the Bolshevik revolt in 1917, the outbreak of the Russo-German War in 1941, the future of Europe and of Scandinavia in particular in the event of a Soviet victory (communist bombers would swoop down over Stockholm in six months), and strained Swedish-German foreign relations. Ribbentrop asked if Folke had any proposal for rectifying the latter. Folke replied that allowing the Swedish Red Cross access to work in German concentration camps would go a long way toward mending fences. Ribbentrop offered his best wishes for a successful meeting with Himmler before abruptly ending the discussion.

Much to Folke's surprise, neither Kaltenbrunner nor Schellenberg nor Ribbentrop stood in the way of Folke meeting Himmler. At 5 p.m. on February 19, 1945, Schellenberg went so far as to pick Folke up and chauffeur him 75 miles north of Berlin to a secluded lakeside SS clinic at Hohenlychen. This picturesque setting in the country-side was where the two faced one another for the first time — just five miles from the women's concentration camp of Ravensbrück.

Folke's first impressions: "Himmler was a modest little man, who looked like a harmless schoolteacher from the country . . . whom one would hardly have noticed if one had met him in the street." Himmler was wearing horn-rimmed spectacles and the green SS uniform without the flashy adornments befitting a man of such rank. Folke's description continues: "He had small, delicate and sensitive hands, which I noticed were well manicured although manicure was forbidden in the SS. He seemed strikingly and amazingly obliging. He displayed traces of humor with a hint of grimness, which he used to relieve the tension. Least of all was there anything diabolical in his appearance. Of the cold hardness in his face, of which I had heard so much, I saw none. In his talk with me he showed himself to be a very lively individual — quite sentimental in his enthusiasm as well. It was a highly remarkable experience to listen to the man who had employed the most scandalous means to send millions of people to death, talking with rapture about the gentlemanly methods of warfare between the Germans and the British in France in the summer of 1944, when action was interrupted in the middle so that both sides could collect their wounded. It was also remarkable to feel his reaction when, towards the end of our discussion, I gave him a 16th-century work on Swedish runestones [raised stones with runic inscriptions] — by a Norwegian, who worked among the prisoners of war in Germany.

I had got a tip that Himmler was especially interested in Norwegian runestones. He was visibly moved. Anyway, he said the friendliness I showed him in this way had made a deep impression on him and that he was grateful I had in this manner elected to give him some pleasure under the present circumstances. . . . Himmler was one of the most complicated people I ever met."

Folke asked: "Isn't it pointless to continue the struggle?" Himmler replied with a stock answer: "Every German will fight like a lion before he gives up." Himmler also sang a familiar tune when asked about the home front. "Perhaps you think it sentimental or even absurd, but I have sworn loyalty to Adolf Hitler, and as a soldier and a German I cannot deny my oath. I owe all I am to Hitler. How can I betray him? I have built the SS on the basis of loyalty; I cannot now abandon that basic principle."

The remainder of the conversation of February 19, 1945, concerned Folke's strictly humanitarian proposition. Fortunately, Folke had primed himself during the days before in the details of earlier proposals that had proved futile. No one wanted a repeat of the fiasco involving Musy and the Jewish inmates at Theresienstadt.

"Is it your idea that Norwegians and Danes in German concentration camps should be taken over to Sweden, where they will be trained as policemen? There are many who have received such training already in your country. Do you really consider that a country is genuinely neutral which acts in that manner?" Himmler asked. Folke wondered aloud as to why the Norwegians and Danes couldn't be interned in Sweden.

Himmler raised a second objection. He asked about compensation, the very issue that had rendered the Swiss efforts so disastrous. To that proposal, Folke responded with a firm no and quickly changed the subject. Folke floated the idea of the Swedish Red Cross being allowed to work inside the concentration camps, particularly among the 13,000 Scandinavians. Himmler scoffed at the number, which he called wildly exaggerated. There couldn't possibly be more than 2,000 to 3,000 Scandinavians in captivity, he claimed. The Reichsführer was deeply disturbed by the idea of Allied armies discovering the deplorable conditions inmates lived in when they liberated the concentration camps. There had to be another avenue that allowed Himmler to show himself in a better light while not subverting Hitler's wishes.

And so Himmler made the following concessions: Folke would be allowed to corral the Norwegian and Danish prisoners into one camp so that they might come under the care of the Swedish Red Cross; Folke would also be allowed to weed out the sick and the elderly among the Scandinavian prisoners and send them home; finally, Folke would be allowed to send all Swedish women (and their children) who had married Germans, but who were now widowed or deserted, to Sweden. Himmler also promised to double-check Folke's figures for imprisoned Scandinavians because, surely, they were inflated.

But Himmler was acting out of duress. The thought of shipping German children to Sweden sickened him. He argued aloud that their fathers would almost certainly "much prefer that they grow up in a German queue [waiting for rationed food] than enjoy asylum in a castle in a country as hostile to Germany as Sweden." Nevertheless, Himmler conceded to the demand. After all this was settled, a general discussion about politics ensued in which Himmler covered much of the same ground as Ribbentrop the day before.

Despite the disparate personalities, the meeting was not without humor. Quite early in the conversation, Himmler had examined Folke's badges, remarking that, "I'm surprised you're only a major." Retorted Folke, "I don't think it's any more surprising than the fact that you're a commander in chief."

And the meeting closed with Himmler asking Folke if he had traveled there in a good car. Upon being reassured that he had, Himmler replied, "That's good. Otherwise the Swedish newspapers might come out with large headlines reading 'War Criminal Himmler Murders Count Bernadotte.'"

And with those final words, Himmler left the room.

CHAPTER EIGHT

Nothing Is Sacred

Folke came away from that first meeting with Himmler buoyed by the concessions he'd received. Although Folke didn't get everything he asked for — such as the movement of prisoners directly from Germany to Sweden — their discussion had gone far more smoothly than expected. And at least Folke would be able to assemble the prisoners in one camp, even if it would be a hastily created one, so that the Swedish Red Cross could more efficiently look after them. In Folke's romanticized version of what would happen next, the prisoners would be picked up almost like schoolchildren on a field trip, with one person per seat on a comfortable bus. They would ride along, shielded from danger by the Red Cross insignia, a universal symbol of peace. They would return to their homes — and soon. But the grim reality of what was really going on inside Germany's concentration camps would obliterate any hope of happily ever after.

At the end of 1944, Hitler called for "total war," a charge no one fully understood. To the Allies, though, the declaration meant that nothing was sacred. Most of the Allied pilots — who by this time were dropping thousands of tons of bombs on Germany every day — knew little if anything of Folke's operation. The only thing they would see when flying overhead would be a bright red "target" on buses amid a sea of destruction. Everything was fair game.

If that weren't risky enough, the area in which Folke's convoy would be able to maneuver was shrinking — and fast. On January 17, 1945, the Soviets paraded into the Polish capital of Warsaw, a battleground since the opening day of fighting, and quickly launched a major offensive westward, plowing through the eastern part of Germany and destroying everything in their wake along the route to their ultimate destination: Berlin. The February Yalta Conference had divided Germany into zones of occupation, but that did not constrain the Allies' ferocious push. U.S. troops reached Czechoslovakia and then parts of Germany. They, too, had their sights set on Berlin.

As the Nazi empire crumbled from its edges inward, tens of thousands in the death camps harnessed their energy for prayer, pleading with God for an end to their ordeal. Instead, the nightmare only grew worse, with many rounded up for death marches in early 1945 as the Germans — in one final sadistic spasm — set out to empty the camps and move their inmates to the German heartland, where they could keep their crimes better hidden. A handwritten note on plain paper signed by Heinrich Himmler and apparently referring to the Dachau concentration camp undercut everything Folke was after: "A handover is out of the question. The camp must be evacuated immediately. No prisoner must be allowed to fall into the hands of the enemy alive."

As distasteful as it was, Folke found himself in league with a devil. Leaving the meeting in Hohenlychen, Himmler made it known that he would dictate the terms of any rescue operation — or it wouldn't happen. It was an uncomfortable alliance for Folke, but he saw it as a necessary evil, as the seriousness of the situation was intensifying by the minute. Even as he cracked bad jokes with Folke, the powerful Himmler, known in Germany as "der treue Heinrich," or "the faithful Heinrich," continued to implement the Nazis' "Final Solution" to the Jewish "problem." The goal, Himmler made crystal clear in a 1943 speech to SS generals, was nothing short of the "annihilation of the Jewish people." It was, he said, a "page of glory in our history [that] has never been written and will never be written . . . [but] we had the moral right, we were obligated to our people to kill this people which wanted to kill us." Two years later, his perspective hadn't changed.

Keeping Hitler from hearing about any agreement with Folke was critical. Folke had secured the support of the Swedish Army for his mission, as well as the invaluable assistance of many others in Sweden, Denmark, Norway, and Germany, but he needed to keep what many would later call the largest humanitarian mission of the Second World War inside Germany under wraps to the extent he could. Swedish newspaper editors had agreed to keep quiet. As Himmler's earlier dealings with Switzerland had proved, these plans would be immediately thwarted if Hitler caught wind of them.

Folke used his powers of persuasion to quickly amass a fleet of vehicles and hundreds of volunteers from the armed forces — all willing to risk their lives — in the port city of Malmö in southern Sweden. But in the first few days of March, just as the rescue mission was set to embark, the internecine politics of wartime diplomacy threatened to torpedo Folke's well-laid plans. Folke got a phone call from Germany with an ominous heads-up: Ernst Kaltenbrunner was plotting against him. Unbeknownst to Folke, the fanatic Hitler loyalist had been fuming over the arrangements Folke had negotiated with Himmler and had informed the Danish representative in Berlin that Folke must have been "extraordinarily naïve" to believe a Swedish Red Cross mission would ever be allowed to gain access to any German concentration camp. Kaltenbrunner argued that outside parties were to be kept at bay and away from the camps at all costs so that Germany's international "prestige" would not be tarnished by any undoubtedly "biased" descriptions of camp conditions. Understanding how influential Kaltenbrunner was — he could have divulged the plan to Hitler at any moment — Folke knew his arrangement was dangerously close to unraveling.

But Folke also knew that the German phone system was tapped, so when he was on the line to Swedish representatives in Berlin, he stated plainly that he would not tolerate any interference with the plan from anyone but Himmler himself. Then, out of an abundance of caution, Folke flew back to Berlin on March 5. And Kaltenbrunner was right there waiting for him. He told Folke that the plan had changed: any scheme to rescue prisoners was now out of the question. But the determined Folke wasn't having it. "I will not allow one of Himmler's underlings to sabotage an agreement which I have myself reached personally with him," he said. Kaltenbrunner would try his best to do just that, but thanks to the intervention of Walter Schellenberg, head of the SS Foreign Intelligence Service, the deal was salvaged. Schellenberg went over Kaltenbrunner's head and confirmed the details of the arrangement with Himmler himself.

And so with the help of the Swedish commander-in-chief, General Helge Jung, Folke's transport column was gathered at Malmö under the leadership of a very capable colonel named Gottfried Björk. In compliance with German orders, it was limited to no more than 300 Swedish soldiers, doctors, and nurses. Their convoy consisted of three platoons of buses, each comprising 12 vehicles, and one platoon of trucks, amounting to 12 more vehicles. They were tasked with nothing less than pulling up outside any camps they could to collect Scandinavian prisoners and bring them back to a holding center at the Neuengamme concentration camp in the north of Germany.

There, they would be able to wait out the war with the support of the Swedish Red Cross before, fingers crossed, being transferred across the Danish border and on to Sweden. Since Folke was not permitted to buy any supplies inside Germany — as all materials had to be set aside for the waning Nazi military campaign — the vehicles had to bring everything with them. This included food and fuel. The buses ran on a mixture of gasoline and ethanol and used a half-liter of fuel per kilometer — a lot of fuel was required. Once the rescues commenced, another monumental challenge would be the prisoners' chronic diarrhea, which meant that the team needed to acquire a large supply of portable toilets that could be utilized during the transports.

The convoy set off over the course of two days, March 9 and 10, since all of them couldn't fit on the ferry from Malmö to Copenhagen at the same time. At first, the buses were painted in camouflage colors in accordance with Swedish army practices, with red crosses and Swedish painted flags on the sides and the roofs. But the evening before the first group was to depart, an order came down from the Swedish Foreign Office, at the insistence of the British, that all vehicles be painted white so that the Allies could easily distinguish them from enemy vehicles — even though there was no guarantee of safety. Folke's people scrambled to get this accomplished but there was little time. Some of the painting actually had to be completed aboard the ferry as it sailed to Denmark. As a result, the rescue mission was known from that point on as the White Buses.

White paint or not, Folke's team was vulnerable and would be strafed by Allied planes in the coming weeks. Many times, someone in the convoy would hear air raid sirens or spot planes flying overhead, causing the drivers to quickly pull over so that everyone on board could scramble off the bus and take cover in a roadside ditch. It later came to light that German trucks were also being painted white, with red crosses, in an effort to try and fool the Allies. Even Folke wasn't immune to the risks. On one journey between Berlin and Hamburg, Folke heard explosions but continued on. Suddenly, he and his driver found themselves directly under six low-flying American planes. "Cold shivers ran down my spine," he said. As Folke hid behind some trees, the Americans dropped a bomb, missing him by only a few hundred yards.

On March 11, the convoy reached Denmark's third-largest city, Odense, on the southern shore of Oresund — the strait that forms the Swedish-Danish border. There, the Danish Red Cross had meals waiting, more than enough for every member of the team, and Folke marveled at the "magnificent hospitality" shown by the Danish authorities. The next day, the convoy crossed the German-Danish border and continued on across the battle-scarred landscape via Kiel, a port city on Germany's Baltic Sea coast, and Lübeck, a northern German city, before finally reaching Friedrichsruh Castle, an estate owned by Prince Otto von Bismarck and his Swedish wife, Ann-Mari, who happened to be an old schoolmate of Folke's. The picturesque Friedrichsruh Castle had been given to Bismarck by Kaiser Wilhelm I, after he defeated France in the Franco-Prussian war of 1870–1871. Friedrichsruh was just east of Hamburg and not far from the border with Denmark. Its storybook loveliness was also only a few miles away from the horrors of Neuengamme, one of the most notorious German concentration camps, which was now slated to be the gathering spot for rescued Scandinavian prisoners from the White Buses mission. Folke arrived at Friedrichsruh on March 9 to await the arrival of the Swedish Red Cross vehicles, which were expected three days later.

Established in December 1938 on the grounds of an abandoned brickworks on the banks of the Dove-Elbe, the Neuengamme camp was surrounded by a double row of electrified barbed wire fencing. Guards were everywhere, at the ready, posted in watch towers and policing the fence lines. Patrols accompanied by fierce dogs roamed further afield in the surrounding terrain, discouraging even the most intrepid of prisoners from attempting escape. The camp commandant, Max Pauly, was a veteran of the extermination system and had earned his stripes by managing the "busiest" gas chambers at other locations. From 1941 to 1942, Pauly was commander of the Stutthof concentration camp, just east of the city of Gdansk, where 68,000 to 85,000 people perished, many of them non-Jewish Poles. At Neuengamme, Pauly's guards were merciless, doling out punches, lashes, and kicks without any regard for a prisoner's health. Anyone even remotely capable of physical labor was ordered to take part in one of 35 external work units forced to clear areas in the surrounding countryside bombed by the Allies. In any given week, unexploded ordnance in the fields took dozens of lives. In these, the final stages of the Holocaust, conditions at Neuengamme were deteriorating by the hour, and work in the fields was only one small part of it. By the end of the war, it was conservatively estimated that more than 52,000 prisoners died there, 28,000 of them during the last six months, when thousands were executed in an effort to stamp out any sign of war crimes and thousands more perished in wretched death marches. In total, the SS incarcerated approximately 104,000 to 106,000 people in Neuengamme from December 1938 until May 1945; approximately 13,500 of the prisoners were women. Initially there were very few Jews, but in the end some 13,000 were imprisoned there.

A 17-year-old American inmate, Phillip Jackson, miraculously survived the ordeal and later testified about it at the war crimes trials: "We were taken out in batches of a hundred and taken to some showers where we were deprived of our clothes and everything else we wore or carried. . . . Our heads and the remainder of our bodies were completely shaved. Then we had a bath, after which a most minute search was made of our naked bodies with lamps. Then we received a most miscellaneous collection of our very old clothes, not even fit for a beggar to wear, and a pair of wooden shoes.

"Food consisted of about one-quarter of a three-pound loaf of black bread and one liter of cabbage or Swede soup per person. . . . Normally we had 500 men sleeping in one block, two to a bed, but often this would increase to 700. Conditions of living were absolutely foul — the stench was awful at night when all the windows were closed.

"[SS Senior Leader] Anton Thumann was constantly going around the camp beating and whipping the prisoners and letting his large unmuzzled dogs loose on the prisoners. I saw this happen many times. One day when we were marching back to the camp I saw him punch my [supervisor] several times in the face because he said our column was not marching in step. He always attended the hanging of people and read the sentences and gave the order to hang."

To assemble and create space for all the incoming prisoners in Neuengamme — where it would rapidly become so jampacked that the Scandinavians were forced to sleep four or five to a bed — the Nazis demanded that the White Buses transport thousands of non-Scandinavians to other concentration camps, all of which were dangerously overcrowded, overflowing with frail or dying inmates. The Germans absolutely refused to set up a separate Scandinavian section or to allow the Swedish delegation in until the prisoners of other nationalities — Dutch, French, Polish, Belgian, and Russian — were reassigned and transported out. Folke and his volunteers found themselves in the unenviable position of having to carry out the Nazis' dirty work, but they moved people out at a fast clip. There was no other choice. But many of those made to leave were perilously thin and suffered from dysentery and other medical issues. Gestapo guards that accompanied the transports would throw the prisoners around like rag dolls and, in time, the Swedes found it nearly impossible to disguise their disgust.

Bertil Bernadotte later said, "All my father wanted to do was get the prisoners near the border so he could quickly get them out when Germany finally collapsed. . . . It was the worst thing to have to take these people to other over-crowded camps and make them even more crowded. They knew they were probably driving them to their death. But there was no alternative."

As soon as a White Bus crossed the German border, a German liaison officer would hop on board. In total, 40 German officers, SS officers, and Gestapo were assigned to Folke's detachment. It was stipulated that every bus should be accompanied by at least one German official. At first, the Swedes were puzzled as to the purpose served by these German officials. But soon they realized the Germans were there not to watch the prisoners but to keep an eye on the Swedish personnel. Swedish records described the initial relationship between Swedes and Germans as cool but cor-dial. But coolness turned to revulsion as the volunteers caught glimpses of emaciated prisoners and dead bodies stacked like firewood. The Swedes had to keep up appearances and play nice, as they were dependent on the Germans for permits to access the various camps. And always it was the Germans who decided where the buses went.

The conditions on the buses were tense. "We had no weapons ourselves, but on most of the buses there was a Gestapo officer," recalled Helge Anderson, one of the bus drivers. "They were dressed in civilian clothes, in suits of various shapes and sizes. The only uniform of clothing was their black, wide-brimmed hat. They carried pistols under their left arm in holsters underneath the jacket. The Gestapo officers who accompanied the buses tried to prevent contact between the relief workers and the prisoners. They demanded, for example, that a curtain be hung in the drivers' cabs, separating the drivers from the rest of the bus. Private conversations were not allowed, radios had to be switched off and the buses' side windows had to be blacked out. But despite all these measures, personal contact between the relief workers and the prisoners did occur. When the prisoners saw our buttered bread, there almost was a mutiny. . . . All eyes were on us and there was a restless atmosphere on the bus. . . . We could understand them so well. They might not have seen a piece of butter in years. We got ready to give each man his slice of buttered bread, but first we had to ask the German . . . guard on the bus for permission to distribute food. He said we should wait until we were underway. . . . When the journey began and I had finished distributing the bread, they kissed my hands. An old man started to cry when he was given his piece of bread."

After arriving in Germany, the initial three Swedish Red Cross detachments were given specific instructions from which they didn't dare deviate. They were authorized by Himmler to fetch about 600 Scandinavians from the Dachau concentration camp north of Munich, 1,600 Danish policemen from various camps northwest of Dresden, and 2,200 Danes and Norwegians from the Sachsenhausen concentration camp north of Berlin. But it was never as easy as driving from point A to point B. There were always obstacles. And then more obstacles.

For example, before the inaugural trip to Sachsenhausen even got off the ground on March 15, Nazi officials demanded that the buses be driven by German drivers when they were within the actual camp area. If not, the prisoners would be forced to walk miles away from the camp to meet the buses. After a frenzied flurry of negotiations, the Swedish drivers were finally permitted to drive the buses one at a time into the camp — but only so long as they had a German guard right beside them. Everywhere they went, the Gestapo escorted the buses to ensure the convoys followed all the instructions precisely — so that no outsider would see too much. Over the course of a few days, 10 trips were made to Sachsenhausen. The agreed-upon timetable had the buses leaving Friedrichsruh at 5 p.m. and arriving at the camp at 1 a.m. — nighttime was deemed safest for traveling to avoid the air raids on Berlin.

Between March 16 and 30, 2,161 prisoners were transported out of Sachsenhausen. On March 19, two other columns left for the south of Germany with a total of 24 buses and 134 men. Their goal was to travel to the camps at Dachau, Mauthausen, and Natzweiler. Five days later, the buses returned to Neuengamme with 313 Danes and 143 Norwegians from Dachau, two Danes and 68 Norwegians from Mauthausen, and 33 Norwegians from Natzweiler. The rescuers were forced to leave behind 67 prisoners who were ill with contagious diseases.

Folke remained in Germany until March 20. He then traveled to Stockholm, where he met with Felix Kersten, Himmler's personal masseur, who was instrumental in making sure Himmler kept his word when it came to his agreement with Folke. A Baltic German, Kersten resided in Stockholm and commuted to Berlin to care for his very famous patient, all of which made him well-positioned to act as a middle man between the Swedish foreign office and Himmler. Unsympathetic to the Nazi cause, Kersten used Himmler's dependence on his treatments to aid various individuals and groups as best he could. With Kersten's assistance, for example, the Swedish foreign office was able to secure the freedom of 50 Norwegian students, 50 Danish policemen, and three Swedes in December 1944.

Folke traveled back again to Germany on March 28. Two days later, on Good Friday, Folke finally was able to finagle his way into the Neuengamme camp, where tens of thousands of people perished in the final months of the war. Driving through the large iron gates with his White Buses and staff, Folke became the first representative of a neutral humanitarian organization to be allowed to inspect a German concentration camp. Previously, Swedish workers who arrived at the concentration camps had been obliged to wait outside the fence for those due to be repatriated.

Even though Folke had made the arrangements directly with Himmler, Himmler did not show up for the prisoner release. Instead, Folke was greeted by a scowling Kaltenbrunner, clearly unhappy about the mission and still suspicious of Folke's motives. As soon as there were no more than a few delegates from the Swedish Red Cross inside Neuengamme, Camp Commander Pauly ordered that the gates be shut behind them.

Folke later called Neuengamme "one of the worst" places he'd ever seen. Pauly permitted Folke to speak only with the Scandinavian prisoners and only in their native tongue. He also severely limited the Swedish party's access to all parts of the camp. Folke agreed to whatever Pauly wanted and said little in order not to arouse suspicion, undermine the release, or endanger the possibility of future talks.

Bertil Bernadotte recalls a story his mother relayed about his father's visit to Neuengamme: "There was a doctor there who was afraid to go into the room where the prisoners with typhus were kept behind closed doors. So when my father got there, he asked the doctor what was in that closed-off room. The doctor told him not to worry about it. But then a nurse spoke up and told my father that the room was where the patients with typhus were kept. My father said, 'Well, let's start with that room then,' and he grabbed the doctor and went inside. The doctor had no choice but to go into that room with my father, who was never afraid of anything."

One prisoner Folke encountered there was someone he had known in America years earlier, a highly regarded Norwegian architect named Odd Nansen. It sickened Folke to see Nansen snatch off his cap and stand to attention, as all prisoners were required to do in the presence of a German of rank.

Years later, Nansen wrote about his time in Neuengamme: "The first thing that hit us . . . was the stench of rubbish and undiluted sewage. We arrived at a medium-sized paved square surrounded by huts fenced off with barbed wire. Behind it, we could see our comrades from the earlier transports. We were called up, lined up in rows of five and finally marched into the barbed-wire enclosure, from where we entered a hut. But what a hut it was! . . . It seemed that the straw and the blankets were alive because of all the lice. It was the same mess everywhere, stench and dirt wherever you looked. Nothing but chaos and misery. Except for us, all inmates were Muselmänner. It was miserable." Muselmänner was camp slang for prisoners who suffered from a combination of starvation and exhaustion and were resigned to their impending death.

When Folke left the camp, he called out to the Danes and Norwegians left behind, "Paa gjensyn" — "goodbye" in Norwegian. He later said: "I saw the joy in their eyes. . . . But I thought, too, of the prisoners of whom I had caught a glimpse in a part of the camp where we had no power. There were thousands of unhappy human beings there, or rather human wrecks, wandering aimlessly about the camp, apathetic, vacant, incapable of ever returning to a normal existence."

More than anything else, though, Folke's visit gave the Scandinavian prisoners a glimmer of hope that their freedom, after so many years, was a possibility. As Vincent Lind, a former prisoner from Denmark, described it: "The next day, things suddenly became very turbulent. People were shouting that the Count [Bernadotte was there]. . . . Somebody from the military came in with Bernadotte. . . . The soldier bowed very low, and afterwards, two women, they were Red Cross nurses, came to us. . . . And I remember that we had forgotten that such people even existed. And suddenly these two women were there. That was so . . . it was an incredible sign of the changes that were to come. And then he greeted us and exchanged a few, very few words with us, turned around and left."

After Folke departed Neuengamme, conditions improved for the Scandinavians there. Swedish Red Cross staff members were allowed to delouse and vaccinate the prisoners against typhus, and the prisoners were able to bathe at least once a week. Even better, the inmates were no longer forced to risk their lives by clearing the fields of bombs. Each was assigned his own bed and was given a clean change of clothes. Soon, the prisoners had received so many Red Cross parcels they actually had more food than they needed — an unusual but good problem to have. According to Odd Nansen, Scandinavian prisoners would hurl extra food over the fence to help their non-Scandinavian fellow prisoners, even though this was strictly forbidden. Danish survivor Per Ulrich remembers, "They would fight over it like wild dogs. It was a terrible sight!"

After coming face-to-face with the evidence of the barbarity at Neuengamme, Folke knew that no matter what, he would have to find a way to expand the mission beyond just the removal of a few thousand Scandinavians from a handful of camps in late March. By April, his contacts in Stockholm agreed that Folke would have to go back to Himmler to persuade him to agree to broaden the mission to include other nationalities. The unprecedented magnitude of this event, with thousands dying each day even as the Allies were blasting through German defenses, meant the Swedes had to act fast. Scared for the future, even lower-level Nazi leaders were determined to destroy everyone and everything so that their brutality might go unnoticed and unpunished. Expediency was everything. And what if Hitler found out?

Folke knew he needed a second meeting with Himmler. Fortunately, he still had something of an ally in the pragmatic Schellenberg, who had been encouraging Himmler to overthrow Hitler and forge his own peace deal with the Allies, using Hitler's worsening health as an excuse. Schellenberg personally traveled to Stockholm in the spring of 1945 to help arrange more meetings between Folke and Himmler.

Bertil Bernadotte said that his father wouldn't have been able to achieve what he did without Schellenberg. "My mother told me that my father often said that Schellenberg, Himmler's closest confidante, helped more than anyone else to persuade Himmler to do what he did," he said. "Schellenberg knew that he had to save his own skin as well because he knew Germany was losing the war and that it was all going to hell in a handbasket."

It was a race against time. A second meeting with Himmler was arranged for April 2 at Hohenlychen once again. Schellenberg was also to be present. Only this time, the adversary Folke encountered would be a completely different man.

CHAPTER NINE

A Ghastly Gamble for Human Lives

One "perk" of Folke's position was that the Nazis allowed him to drive pretty much anywhere he wanted on the public roads, at a time when travel was carefully monitored and restricted. It was on one of these drives from Schönhausen — the Baroque manor west of Berlin where some members of the Swedish Legation were stationed — when he got his first look at women prisoners from concentration camps. The image would forever be seared into his memory. There were Jewish women. There were German women accused of working against the Nazis. There were German and foreign women imprisoned as communists, prostitutes, abortionists, or some other kind of "deviant."

For the most part, these women had entered the camps in adequate physical condition, which helped them weather the daily abuse and brutality inflicted by the guards. But as these survivors walked in single file along the side of the road to their "jobs" — they were all working as slave labor — their slow gait, gaunt cheeks, hunched shoulders, skeletal figures, and dull eyes belied any pretense of decent health. Many were dehydrated. Some were anemic. Malnutrition was rampant. Their exhaustion was total. This was the slave workforce that German manufacturers — Siemens in particular, as well as Daimler-Benz — paid handsomely to access. When a woman reached the end of her usefulness, her energy sucked dry, she was sent back to the camp, and she stayed there — until she died or was killed.

Jockeying with the women for space on the roads were hordes of refugees, marching in whichever direction seemed safer than where they were before. During the icy winter of 1944–1945, nearly 750,000 refugees attempted to escape from the front as the Soviets advanced toward East Prussia. Along the way, some 300,000 people would freeze or starve to death or be strafed by aircraft as they lumbered along with nowhere to go. Some refugees concocted a kind of crude train, using farm wagons to carry whatever possessions they'd somehow managed to hold on to. Often the burden was too great for the horses, and they would collapse, only to be dragged to the side so the ongoing stream could struggle on.

Every so often, Allied aircraft would pop up in the sky, seemingly out of nowhere, and the noise of exploding bombs would send refugees scrambling to take cover in ditches by the side of the road. But by early 1945, some no longer bothered even looking up when they heard the roar of approaching aircraft. They just kept plodding on, as if nothing was happening, seeming to care not a whit whether they survived.

"When we passed these unfortunates, weeks had gone by since they had abandoned their homes. They were being directed to different centers where the local authorities would be responsible for their billeting and feeding. They appeared worn and weary, and utterly hopeless," Folke later wrote. "There was no future for them, and the present was an inferno. Whatever they had possessed was lost, material goods as well as any belief in life. Silently the pitiable procession moved on, along roads lined with the carcasses of emaciated horses who had pulled the primitive vehicles until their strength gave out. These vehicles were similar to the 'covered wagons' used by the early settlers in America."

All of this unleashed an even greater resolve on Folke's part to forge ahead as quickly as possible with an expansion of the rescue operation as he set out to meet Himmler a second time on April 2. It had been only a few weeks since their first meeting, but this time the Nazi leader appeared to have shed most of his bravado. Indeed, Himmler seemed fretful and nervous — completely different from the defiant man Folke had first encountered. Himmler was quick to emphasize that he wouldn't go back on his "binding" oath to Hitler, and he vowed to continue with the war because that's what Hitler wanted. But he certainly didn't look like a man whose heart was still in the fight.

"You should think about doing something more than being loyal to Hitler if you [believe] that Hitler's decision to continue the war is a disaster for your country," Folke told him. "A person in your position, with an indescribable responsibility such as you have, cannot blindly follow his leader but must have the courage to answer for the consequences."

Himmler was then called out of the room, which gave Schellenberg the chance to pose the direct question he'd been itching to ask, "Couldn't you go to Eisenhower and discuss with him the possibility of capitulation on the western front?"

"That's impossible," Folke replied. "The initiative must come from Himmler. If I made myself available, it would be interpreted in Allied circles that I believed Eisenhower and the governments of the western powers were prepared to enter into negotiations for an armistice. I am absolutely convinced that is not the case."

When Himmler returned, Folke raised the stakes in this ghastly gamble for human lives. He restated his desire for permission to transport the assembled prisoners at Neuengamme to Denmark and then onward to Sweden. At first, Himmler balked, explaining that there simply was too great a risk that Hitler would find out. But then Himmler's long-held resolve began to waver. He offered an alternative, suggesting that "some" of the assembled prisoners could be released, as letting everyone go at once would draw too much attention.

Folke lobbed another risky salvo, asking that all Danish and Norwegian women and sick Scandinavian men be allowed to go to Sweden — as well as a portion of the 461 Norwegian students in Neuengamme. Surprisingly, Himmler nodded in agreement. Those in need of medical attention would be allowed to travel to hospitals in Denmark. But he emphasized that they absolutely could not proceed on to any other country until after the war was over. Himmler consented as well to the release of a number of French citizens whose names Folke had compiled.

This bizarre humanitarian tit-for-tat lasted a good four

hours, but there was no further mention of capitulation. On the way back to Berlin, however, Schellenberg told Folke that Himmler hadn't given up on the idea and had continued discussing the terms of a surrender after Folke had left the meeting. If not for Hitler, Himmler would never have hesitated to ask Folke himself to proceed to Eisenhower to propose a surrender on the western front. It was clear Himmler remained greatly torn by his desire to save Germany from complete destruction and his devotion to his boss. But the veneer of loyalty was starting to crack. Like so many Germans, Himmler and Schellenberg were worried about the lawless Red Army advancing on the eastern front amid reports of a rampage of looting and killing that went far beyond collateral damage. The victorious Russians were committing a staggering number of unspeakable criminal acts, and many Nazi leaders were genuinely afraid.

Before returning to Stockholm on April 9, Folke saw Schellenberg again. The latter said that Himmler had continued flirting with the idea of negotiating a separate peace on the western front, with Folke acting as an intermediary between Himmler and Eisenhower. This time, Folke didn't immediately say no. Rather he told Schellenberg that he would do it, but only if Himmler stated publicly that Hitler had tapped Himmler to lead the German people in the event of Hitler's illness or death. Folke also would need an official guarantee that all — and not just some — Scandinavian prisoners would be sent to Sweden. In addition, Himmler would have to put an end to Operation Werwolf, his plan to use an elite guerrilla force to slow down the Allied advance and buy more time for negotiation. Folke didn't believe Himmler would go for it, but Schellenberg promised to do his best to persuade him.

Despite Kaltenbrunner's attempt to thwart him at every turn, Folke kept touring the country as best he could, stopping by concentration camps to ascertain the most effective way to rescue the remaining prisoners. Unabashedly proud of his successes so far, Folke showed his mettle by turning up unexpectedly at Neuengamme to ask that future releases include Jews. On April 17, he wrote to officials back in Stockholm with some good news: "Today I can announce that 423 Jews are expected to arrive tomorrow in Sweden, where they are to remain until the end of the war." Those prisoners were from Theresienstadt. Two days later, additional Scandinavian prisoners were ferried out of Neuengamme. Before long, 4,225 of Neuengamme's Scandinavian inmates would be carted away on buses, the first step on the path to freedom. The Swedish government couldn't have been more pleased with these accomplishments.

But then came April 19. During a visit to the Danish-German border, Folke was told that Himmler had suddenly closed the door on any further attempts to transport Scandinavian prisoners from Neuengamme to Sweden via Denmark. The following day, Folke learned that an order also had gone out at Neuengamme — all prisoners were to be evacuated immediately. What was going on? It wasn't long before Folke found out. Himmler was outraged over the negative publicity that had followed the Allies' discovery of the morbid conditions at Buchenwald and Bergen-Belsen concentration camps. He told Folke: "That those camps, which according to my information were in the best shape, should have become the object of such disgraceful descriptions is really shocking. Nothing has hit me so hard as the Allied Press accounts in this connection."

Bergen-Belsen was the first main concentration camp that fell into British hands — and the first camp to be widely known to the public. When troops turned up there on April 15, they were horrified to discover 38,000 prisoners barely alive, with no food, water, or sanitary facilities. Even more disturbing were the more than 10,000 rotting corpses piled so high on the camp's grounds that bulldozers had to be used to shove them into mass graves. Himmler had no idea that the British would film and photograph the heaps of dead bodies or that the film would be shown in movie theaters around the world. One of those who died at Bergen-Belsen, Anne Frank, lies in an unmarked grave there, the victim of a typhus epidemic.

Adding more urgency to the situation at Bergen-Belsen was that, by now, American troops were pouring into Europe, reaching Czechoslovakia, which would be liberated by U.S. forces in May 1945. "This is not the hour of final victory," said President Harry S. Truman, in office only days since Roosevelt had died of a stroke on April 12, 1945. "But the hour draws near, the hour for which all the American people, all the British people and all the Soviet people have toiled and prayed so long."

But Hitler remained undeterred, blustering with fake confidence, ordering that any and all retreating Nazi officers be shot.

*

All of this set the stage for a final frenzy of negotiations.

Folke returned to Berlin on April 20, the last birthday Hitler would live to see. By this time, the sounds of artillery booming in the distance had grown so loud that it was impossible for anyone to ignore the fact that the advancing Soviet Army was just days away from storming the city. The drive that day between Friedrichsruh and Berlin was particularly nerve-wracking. The war in the air had by then grown so intense that Folke had finally agreed to take extra precautions while on the road. He hired two chauffeurs, one of whom was positioned on the trunk at the back of the car so that he could act as an alarm. Anytime he saw Allied planes approaching, he was to signal the others by banging a stick on the top of the car. The driver would then know to stop so that everyone could scurry out and take cover.

Passing through the town of Nauen, 26 miles west of Berlin, Folke looked for and spotted blue and yellow flags, a signal that an air raid was on, but nothing serious seemed to be happening, so they carried on to the outskirts of town. "Seeing an old woman by the side of the road we pulled up, and I asked her if a raid was on. Before she had time to reply, we heard the dull drone of a large number of Allied bombers. A few seconds later bombs were dropped on the railway station, less than a hundred yards away," Folke later wrote. "We drove on out of the town and took cover in a trench which had been dug at the side of the road for the defense of the adjoining village, the plan apparently being to sweep the road with anti-tank guns."

For about an hour, Folke and his chauffeurs holed up in the ditch. They could actually see the bombs as they left the planes, and follow them as they turned into white columns of smoke that rushed toward and crashed into the ground at incredible speed. An ear-splitting explosion always followed. "This was the first time I observed anything approaching panic among the German population. A crowded shelter had been hit, a number of people killed, and men and women came running across the fields, aimlessly seeking shelter in ditches and anything that offered cover of any kind," Folke wrote. "It was as if the people of Nauen felt that nothing could save them, since not even a few fighters from the nearby airfield of Spandau came up to engage the enemy."

Once in Berlin, Folke reached out to the always ready Schellenberg, who arranged for Folke to meet Himmler the following morning for breakfast. At this third meeting, Himmler looked even more worn out and worried, nervously drumming his fingers on the table. Sensing that Folke was watching him closely, Himmler felt compelled to explain that he hadn't slept in over 24 hours. The day before, he'd been with Hitler in his Berlin bunker for a celebration, albeit a dreary one, of the Nazi leader's 56th birthday. Besides Himmler, the other members of Hitler's dwindling inner circle who were present included Joseph Goebbels, Hermann Göring, Joachim von Ribbentrop, Albert Speer, and Martin Bormann. In between half-hearted champagne toasts, Hitler received birthday wishes with a blank stare. Benito Mussolini had sent a congratulatory telegram. (Only a few days later, Mussolini would be captured and executed by Italian partisans.)

The group urged Hitler to get out of Berlin and to relocate to the relative safety of Berghof, Hitler's beloved chalet in the

Bavarian Alps. Around it were several mountain homes for members of the Nazi leadership, along with a landing strip and other facilities for security and support staff. From there he could continue fighting the good fight, they argued, only this time he could be supported by troops positioned throughout the impenetrable Alpine mountains of western Austria and southern Bavaria. Hitler's cohorts presented a positive facade, reasoning that such a move might prolong the war so that the odds could be tipped in Germany's favor. But Hitler wasn't buying it. There was absolutely no way he would venture out of his underground sanctuary and risk capture by his enemies, who would no doubt publicly humiliate him in the worst ways possible.

It was bizarre for Folke to arrive in Berlin on Hitler's birthday, which in other years had been celebrated with great gusto by legions of devoted subjects. Ever since 1933, when it was made a major German holiday, military parades and other massive events marked the occasion each year. Hitler's milestone 50th birthday in 1939 was said to be one factor that convinced him he was running out of time and so should go to war in order to achieve his goals. Now Berlin had become a silent city, a shell of what it had been. Those who remained wandered about aimlessly, with no idea of what was going to happen next, let alone that it was Hitler's birthday.

Sitting across from Himmler, Folke told him about how shocked he'd been when he first came across the pathetic sight of frail women prisoners walking along the sides of the road. Folke asked him, "Isn't it terrible about these women who have been torn from their homes?" Himmler just sat there and said nothing. But when Folke ventured to request the release of women from Ravensbrück, Himmler started to squirm. Although Himmler still prohibited Scandinavian prisoners in Denmark to continue on to Sweden, he finally consented to the Swedish Red Cross retrieving all French women imprisoned at Ravensbrück. He didn't even mind if women of other nationalities there were removed as well, since they were already about to be "evacuated" — possibly a euphemism for murder.

It was a stunning concession. Until that meeting, Himmler had banned Folke from rescuing anyone incarcerated at Ravensbrück. But Himmler knew that if the world was shocked by the conditions of camps holding men, they would be even more horrified by the treatment of the women. Nazi officials were so afraid of how the public would react that in the days before Ravensbrück was liberated, every prisoner's file was burned, along with as many bodies as possible. The ashes were tossed into the lake.

At the time, Folke had little inkling of what the 30,000 female inmates still at the Ravensbrück camp endured. Not only were they singled out for inhumane medical experiments, many also suffered sexual assaults by Nazi soldiers. Although the camp was in the firing line of the advancing Allied troops, the gas chambers were still in heavy use. People were fleeing Berlin in droves and buildings were being flattened by bombs, creating a moonscape of craters, and yet all that anybody cared about at Ravensbrück was that the women who could no longer perform manufacturing jobs be exterminated — and fast. The plan was to kill those who weighed less than 85 pounds as well as anyone who was too sick or weak to work.

Indeed, during the last few weeks of the war, more than 6,000 women were gassed at Ravensbrück, while others were shot, starved, or forced out on death marches. The commandant of Ravensbrück was Fritz Suhren, whose policy was to kill prisoners not only with the help of the gas chamber — which was built and operated on Suhren's watch — but also by grinding them down through hard physical labor with almost no nutrition. Suhren kept the office of Dr. Karl Gebhardt well-stocked with testing material. Gebhardt, one of Himmler's personal physicians, conducted horrific surgical experiments on prisoners during the war. For example, he broke the legs of Ravensbrück inmates and infected them with various organisms in order to test certain drugs in treating gas gangrene.

Exactly how much Folke knew about what was going on with the women there we don't know, but he continued to push forward with a rescue operation, whether on Himmler's terms or not, no matter what compromises had to be made.

Ravensbrück had been established by Himmler as a place for women deemed inferior — women the Nazis wanted out of the gene pool. He handpicked the camp's location not only because it was hidden but also for its beautiful setting. It didn't hurt that one of his best friends in the Gestapo had a country house in the area so that he could visit the camp and his friends in one trip. Himmler believed that nature was essential for strengthening German genes: Germans would grow up stronger than everyone else, like the trees in the woods, if surrounded by the pristine loveliness of the great outdoors.

The camp received its first 867 female inmates in May 1939. Another 130,000 would pour in before it was all over. Ravensbrück was designed to hold no more than 3,000 people, but at its peak, in February 1945, it held 46,473 women from more than 30 countries. The "inferior beings" — social outcasts, political enemies, the sick, disabled, and insane — were held hostage in the camp by armed guards and a high wall with electrified barbed wire. Many of the women were allowed out to serve as slave labor, helping manufacture weapons, munitions, and explosives. Only a few dared try to escape.

Over the years, Himmler made frequent trips to Ravensbrück. He barked orders each time he stopped by. On one occasion, he demanded that the cooks add more root vegetables to the prisoners' soup. Another time, he told guards to pick up the pace of the executions.

But now, for whatever reason, Folke was able to convince Himmler to allow the Swedish Red Cross to rescue at least some of the prisoners at Ravensbrück. After breakfast the following morning, the same day the Russians tore through the outer Berlin defenses, Folke hurried off to Friedrichsruh, which served as a headquarters for the White Bus mission to secure the evacuation of the Ravensbrück prisoners. From there he traveled over the German border to Padborg, Denmark, to meet with the Danish Red Cross to determine the agency's capacity for coping with a new influx of female prisoners.

In the end, the Ravensbrück rescue effort was far more difficult and dramatic than anything Folke could have imagined. On paper, it was a simple enough plan. Twenty-five white Swedish buses, each marked with a red cross, would drive to Ravensbrück. There would be doctors along as well as three nurses (one of them was Folke's sister, Countess Maria Bernadotte). But the operation was anything but easy. In February 1948, at Schellenberg's war trial, Franz Göring, a liaison between Himmler and Folke's rescue workers, described what he witnessed when he drove to the Ravensbrück concentration camp in the spring of 1945. Upon arrival, Göring estimated the prison's population included about 9,000 Polish women and about 1,500 women from France, Belgium, Holland, and other countries, in addition to approximately 3,000 Jewish women. He talked with the camp commandant, Suhren, about how best to evacuate them all. Göring suggested the women begin marching by foot to Malchow — one of Ravensbrück's numerous sub-camps — where a column of Red Cross buses would be waiting. Suhren agreed, promising that he'd send the women on their way later that same day. No problem. But when Göring arrived in Malchow, no one knew what he was talking about. Prisoners were supposed to be arriving from Ravensbrück? Not according to anyone Göring encountered.

"We then drove back to Ravensbrück and confirmed for ourselves that Suhren had in fact not sent the women on their march as agreed. When I asked him why he had failed to keep his end of the agreement, he answered . . . that in accordance with the führer's orders, the prisoners had to remain in the camp," said Göring, who then tracked down Rudolf Brandt, Himmler's personal assistant. "I described the situation to Dr. Brandt and requested an immediate decision from Himmler. Not long afterward, Dr. Brandt called back and ordered Suhren to release the prisoners for evacuation as agreed. Suhren then declared to me in private that he was now completely at a loss, since he had explicit orders from Nazi leaders to liquidate the women if enemy troops were ever to approach. Suhren now became very uncertain and confided to me that he had a group of women in the camp whom he had likewise been explicitly ordered to eliminate: 54 Polish and 17 French women, on whom experiments had been conducted. When I asked him what sort of experiments, he explained that the women in question had been inoculated with bacilli, which had developed into a disease, which in turn had been cured through surgery, partly through muscle surgery, partly through bone surgery. Thereupon I had two of the women brought before me and was convinced of what Suhren had told me. I immediately pointed out to Suhren that he could not, under any circumstances, carry out the order Kaltenbrunner had given until he had received a decision from Himmler. In Lübeck, I contacted Dr. Brandt once again and apprised him of this matter, requested that he obtain a decision from Himmler as soon as possible, and further indicated that these women ought not to be eliminated under any circumstances, especially since the women who were about to be released knew of the experiments. The experiments were known in the camp under the code name Kaninchen (Rabbit). About two hours later I received word from Dr. Brandt that Himmler had ordered the release of the so-called Versuchskaninchen (guinea pigs). Dr. Arnoldson of the Swedish Red Cross, whom I briefed on the whole affair, personally supervised the evacuation of these women."

In the end, about 7,500 women — an estimated 1,000 of them Jews — were liberated from Ravensbrück and its sub-camps between April 22 and 28. Among the first prisoners freed was Nelly Langholm, a Norwegian who had been in the camp for two years. "We couldn't believe it," she later recalled. "We had to walk to the gates. We saw the buses and there were these Swedish men in gray uniforms with red crosses on their arms. I think they told us, 'Now you will go to Sweden. Now you will be free. Can you imagine?'" Langholm recalled being watched by the other prisoners as she walked out, and the guilt she felt about leaving them behind, especially as there were rumors the camp was to be blown up by either the Germans or the Russians. "It was terrible going through Germany. These terrible ruins," she said. "A big town like Hamburg. I don't think I saw a house. We heard the shooting from the West and the Russians from the other side."

Also among the rescued prisoners was Manya Moszkowicz, the teenager from Sosnowiec. She and the other women were transported to Copenhagen and then ferried to Malmö in Sweden. Still wearing their striped prisoner uniforms, they walked slowly off the boat and down the gangplank "all in thin rags, shoes made of paper and wood and odds and ends," wrote one reporter. More women followed, stunned and disbelieving. Some carried Red Cross boxes; some balanced those boxes with babies. Many were too ill to walk and were brought out on stretchers. Upon being approached by white-coated Swedish doctors, more than one survivor suffered hallucinations. According to media reports, they cried out, "I don't want to burn. I don't want to burn," imagining their Nazi tormenters were present. Manya later recalled the fear she felt even after the rescue — she still associated showers with gas chambers. "When we went to bathe, none of us wanted to get into the showers," she said. "A member of the Red Cross turned on the water and got in to show us that it was safe."

It would take time, but in the coming weeks, the women slowly got their strength back as they soaked up all the care they could get. They recuperated in various locations, after which most of the non-Jewish women returned to their homelands. Many of the Jewish women searched high and low for surviving family members, ultimately immigrating to Israel or America, sometimes with family and sometimes without them. They were the lucky ones. When the Allies liberated Ravensbrück on April 29 and 30, they found 3,500 dangerously ill prisoners and many others who were already dead. As the women in Malmö began absorbing all that had transpired, they got word of the man who had initiated their rescue: Folke Bernadotte. They would forever call the kind-looking Swede their savior.

At 3 a.m. the morning of April 23, Folke was startled by the ringing of his phone. On the line was a Nazi official, telling him Schellenberg needed to see him immediately about a matter of great urgency. Folke went to Schellenberg, who dropped a bombshell: Hitler's time was up. He was in such a poor physical state — and in even worse shape mentally — that no one expected him to live longer than another day or two. According to Schellenberg, Himmler wanted to meet with Eisenhower as soon as possible to express his willingness to order German troops to surrender. He asked

Folke if he would take that message to Eisenhower. But Folke thought it wiser to have Himmler's wishes relayed to the Swedish government, which then could pass them on to Allied leaders. Schellenberg understood. He called Himmler and arranged a meeting with Folke in Lübeck, a major seaport 200 miles north of Berlin, for later that night.

As he headed out, Folke recalled later, "I shall not easily forget that night with its uncanny feeling of disaster."

CHAPTER TEN

Hitler's Demise

On the night of April 23, when Folke met with Himmler in Lübeck, it was for the last time. At this point, a visit to the capital, very nearly penned in by Allied troops, was a lethal proposition. More than 2.5 million energized Soviet troops were staring down one million exhausted German fighters, including about 45,000 youth and elderly soldiers who had no business being on a battlefield. Not only were the Germans greatly outnumbered, but they also lacked tanks, planes, and artillery. But that didn't stop the German command from pulling troops tightly around Berlin for a final, doomed defense of the city. There were still plenty of Nazis willing to give their very last breath to fight off their enemies.

By this time, countless Berliners, including a man named Claus Fuhrmann, had already spent weeks out of sight in cellars. He described those final hours before the Soviets completely swarmed the city: "We could not tell whether it was night or day. The Russians drew nearer; they advanced through the underground railway tunnels, armed with flamethrowers; their advance snipers had taken up positions quite near us; and their shots ricocheted off the houses opposite. Exhausted German soldiers would stumble in and beg for water — they were practically children. I remember one with a pale, quivering face who said, 'We shall do it all right; we'll make our way to the north west yet.' But his eyes belied his words and he looked at me despairingly. What he wanted to say was, 'Hide me, give me shelter. I've had enough of it.' I should have liked to help him; but neither of us dared to speak. Each might have shot the other as a 'defeatist.' The scourge of our district was a small one-legged Hauptscharführer [high-ranking member of the SS] who stumped through the street on crutches, a machine pistol at the ready followed by his men. Anyone he didn't like the look of, he instantly shot. The gang went down cellars at random and dragged all the men outside, giving them rifles and ordering them straight to the front. Anyone who hesitated was shot. The front was a few streets away. At the street corner diagonally opposite our house, Walloon Waffen SS [a collaborationist volunteer unit] had taken up position; wild desperate men who had nothing to lose and who fought to their last round of ammunition. Armed Hitler Youth were lying next to men of the Vlassov White Russian Army."

In April, a series of rapidly unfolding events portended Germany's unconditional surrender. Early in the month, Allied forces pushed through the German defensive line in Italy with the help of 1.5 million men and women deployed in the country. Then, on April 25, East met West on the River Elbe, with Soviet and American troops coming together near Torgau, Germany, about 85 miles from Berlin, effectively cutting the country in two. Meanwhile, in northern Italy, Benito Mussolini's puppet government had been dissolved, as Italian partisans and American forces ended German control of the region. On April 27, the 61-year-old Italian dictator and his 33-year-old mistress, Clara Petacci, were captured. The next day, they were executed, their bodies hung by the feet in Piazzale Loreto, a major town square in Milan, where a crowd of fuming Italians spit on and beat the remains.

Hitler was still holed up in his bunker in Berlin, where he had lived since January 16, too scared of capture to stick his head out even for a minute. Encased in 16 feet of concrete and six feet of earth, Hitler's sanctuary protected him physically but still didn't mask the sounds of Soviet shells falling closer by the hour. By now, Hitler had started contemplating his suicide. Himmler was one of the few aware of Hitler's threats to take his own life.

At almost midnight on April 23, Folke greeted Himmler at the Swedish Consulate in Lübeck. Before they'd even started talking, air raid sirens blared, as if on cue. Folke asked Himmler if he wanted to retreat to the bomb shelter. He hesitated no more than a second before saying yes. They joined a small group of Swedes and Germans already huddled there, and Himmler immediately began to talk with the Germans, a veiled attempt to gauge public sentiment. During the hour or so they were there, Folke noticed, no one seemed to recognize Himmler. He also took stock of Himmler's appearance and demeanor. "He struck me as being utterly exhausted and in a very nervy state, and looked as if he were exerting all his willpower to preserve an appearance of inward calm," he later wrote. It was about 1 a.m. when the sirens shrieked again, indicating it was safe to leave the shelter. By this time, the electricity had gone out, so the two men spoke their final words to one another in a conference room by candlelight.

Himmler spoke first: "It is very probable that Hitler is already dead and, if not, he very probably will be within the next few days. The führer has gone to Berlin to perish with its inhabitants. Berlin is surrounded and it is only a matter of days until it falls. The last three times we three have met [Schellenberg was there, too] you urged me to end the war. I agreed with you that the situation was hopeless, that the war must stop, and that Germany must admit she is beaten. But I have not been able to see how I could break my oath to the führer. Now the situation is different. Most probably Hitler is dead. . . . I recognize that Germany is defeated."

Folke remained silent while Himmler rationalized his contemplated insubordination. Folke had always characterized Hitler as cowardly, afraid to take responsibility for his actions. He did not have the courage to try to aid his country in defeat. He was not a leader; he was a man worthy only of contempt. He lacked the gumption to even face his own people, let alone the world. Himmler did not need to justify betraying his führer.

Himmler chattered on nervously, unable to disguise his desperation to negotiate with Allied leaders. He dangled a carrot in front of Folke: permission to spirit any concentration camp prisoners he liked out of the country to the destinations of his choosing. And what did Himmler want in return? Folke's delivery of a message to the Swedish government to be forwarded on to Eisenhower. Wanting to deflect blame, Himmler said he could coordinate the surrender of

German troops at the western front so that they could shift eastward to fight the Soviets. He was mistakenly optimistic that the Americans and British would want to combine their military might with that of the Germans against the Soviets, who were coming to dominate a large portion of Europe. Himmler had even penned a letter to Eisenhower — his own personal olive branch — to make the case that would be ultimately rejected; for the Allies, nothing was acceptable but a complete and unconditional surrender on all fronts.

Folke refused to ferry a message to anyone unless Himmler agreed to complete capitulation in Denmark and Norway, where hundreds of thousands of German troops were embedded, armed, and ready to continue the fight. Himmler agreed to this. Folke then asked that King Leopold of the Belgians, who had for years been a prisoner of the Germans, be freed. The Nazis had thought Leopold might one day prove useful as a hostage. Again, Himmler agreed. Leopold would be released. Folke wasn't about to stop now. He pushed his luck even further by asking for a halt to executions of imprisoned Danish patriots. Himmler agreed again.

Just after 2 a.m., the men left the meeting. Himmler insisted on driving himself but then promptly crashed his car into a barbed wire fence. It took some effort for the two of them to free the ensnared vehicle. "Symbolic," thought Folke, who would never see Himmler again.

Before leaving for Sweden via Denmark with Himmler's capitulation offer in hand, Folke again checked in with Schellenberg. Schellenberg said Himmler was already blathering on about how he should behave upon meeting Eisenhower. Should he bow? Should he shake hands? Himmler wasn't sure. Of course, both Folke and Schellenberg knew there was no chance of such a meeting ever taking place. Relaying a message to the Swedish government committed Folke to nothing. And he also knew America and Britain would never accept a separate armistice with Germany.

Folke then traveled to Copenhagen and informed the Swedish minister there of what had happened during his meeting with Himmler, and then Folke returned to Stockholm the night of April 24. He submitted a report to the Swedish Foreign Minister Christian Günther, and the secretary of the cabinet, Erik Boheman, which traveled up through the appropriate channels before finally making its way onto President Harry Truman's desk. As expected, Truman responded to Himmler's proposal with this: "A German capitulation would only be acceptable on one condition: that it took place on all fronts." The next day, Folke was off to Odense, Denmark, to let Schellenberg know about Truman's reply. Schellenberg sought to arrange a fifth meeting with Himmler, at Lübeck, but that never came to fruition.

Behind the scenes, the rescue operation was still in full swing. On April 22, a column of 15 ambulances left Ravensbrück, packed with sick women prisoners. The next day, a second column of 25 vehicles took off. More women were picked up by still another column on April 24. The women whisked out of Ravensbrück between April 22 and 28 were transported to Denmark and then on to Sweden. There, they received food, clothing, and medical care before being sent on to various locations to recuperate.

But the rescues were getting riskier. With the Soviets ratcheting up their final offensive against the capital, only

50 miles south of Ravensbrück, the Red Army could turn up at the front gate at any time. Ostensibly, the Soviets would liberate the camp, but stories of Russian soldiers raping survivors were common. Many wanted to reward themselves at the expense of the defeated enemy. And few Russians believed that any of those liberated deserved sympathy. Fortunately, the Soviet commanders opted to complete their encirclement of Berlin before eventually heading on to Ravensbrück on April 29 and 30. By that time, only about 2,000 or so sick men, women, and children remained. The White Buses had succeeded in transporting thousands to Denmark through the ever-narrowing corridor between the Soviet front in the east and the British front in the west. Increasingly, the vehicles met with low-flying aircraft charged with strafing German roads.

On the evening of April 24, a column led by Liuetenant Gösta Hallquist arrived in Ravensbrück, where it collected 706 women of different nationalities and headed straight for Denmark. The column spent the night in a forest and divided in two the next day. An Allied fighter plane attacked. It's not clear how many people were killed; the driver died, and Hallquist was badly injured. Several women, too, were killed. The other column, which took a different road, was also attacked, and several prisoners were killed or injured. Despite the danger, the rescues continued. Again and again, Folke ordered the buses to return to Ravensbrück. An American consular official in Stockholm expressed his amazement at the success of the mission, saying "The job being done by the Swedes in caring for the far less fortunate people is nothing short of a miracle."

Folke himself was caught in bombing or heavy strafing at least seven times between mid-February and the end of April. One challenge all the convoys faced was that — at this late stage of the war — maps were of little use. Road signs and fuel stations were almost nonexistent. Mixed-up routes and street names were common. All this led many German officers to inadvertently — or purposefully — misdirect the Swedish drivers. Each Red Cross convoy had to make its own repairs and carry its own fuel. It was a breathless business. "The mission was operating in a very quickly shrinking corridor, being squeezed between the Russians and the Western Allies," Bertil Bernadotte said. "Driving — often in the dark — without any road signs, [and with] blown-up bridges and impassable ruined towns. And with time running out." He later described it as a "James Bond situation."

But everyone kept at it. What was uncovered at the Bergen-Belsen concentration camp in northern Germany on April 15 by Allied troops was the same grim discovery uncovered by Folke's volunteers in camp after camp. The stench of burning flesh. Dead bodies with arms and legs that looked like broomsticks. Those barely alive, wandering around like zombies in striped pajamas, begging for food, water, and cigarettes. This was all the momentum members of the team needed to keep coming back so that as many people as possible could be rescued.

As they lined up in the woods surrounding Ravensbrück, the female prisoners still feared selection for death. When one Dutch woman, Jean Bommezin de Rochement, heard her name called out, she panicked, certain she was about to be gassed. She wrote in her diary, "We leave the camp in the direction of the gas chambers. We move forward and for many of us this is too much. They are seized by a nervous fit . . . we have to drag them forward. . . . We move and see the back of the camp — here are the stores, there is Siemens. Some of the inmates appear behind the windows and the barbed wire looking at us. They know that 'transport' usually means death." At last, Jean found herself moving toward men who smiled "with tears in their eyes as they see us. Suddenly we are about to mount the buses and there is a scramble for places."

Jean's convoy moved off, but amid an Allied air assault the women were forced to quickly get off the buses, according to a *Newsweek* magazine report. "We are too slow to take cover . . . and suddenly we are machine gunned. For a moment, I taste the bitter irony of being killed by our own Allies on the road to freedom but they are gone and I live. Looking around I see a terrible scene. Behind me a woman is bleeding to death," she said. Later, reports revealed that 17 Ravensbrück women died in that convoy and that RAF planes were responsible. The British ambassador in Stockholm voiced "regret" but reminded the Swedes that there had never been any guarantee of "safe passage." Other convoys were hit, but Folke's buses continued to arrive and the women continued to mob them, as rumors circulated that the SS would eventually destroy the camp. Every day, Swedish drivers who reached Ravensbrück predicted their convoy would be the last, as the roads were becoming nearly impassable. And yet buses kept coming.

Meanwhile, what Folke didn't realize when meeting with Himmler was just how much Hitler's bunker was convulsing with chaos and consternation. On April 22, Hitler had convened a three-hour military conference in his dank catacomb, during which he let loose a scathing tirade against the Army and the "universal treason, corruption, lies and failures" of all those who had deserted him. Every day, Hitler continued to issue orders to defend Berlin to troops who were already exhausted, wiped out, or hurrying westward to surrender to the Americans. Joining Hitler in the bunker were propaganda minister Joseph Goebbels and his family, including six young children; top aide Martin Bormann; two of Hitler's secretaries; a handful of military aides; and Hitler's longtime companion Eva Braun. Everyone else had shown their "disloyalty" by fleeing to homes around Hitler's retreat in the Alps.

On April 23, Hitler met with his friend Albert Speer, minister of armaments, for the final time. Speer admitted to his longtime confidante and leader that, in an effort to preserve the country's factories and industry for the postwar period, he had basically thwarted Hitler's order for the systematic destruction of Germany. To this, Hitler sat stoic. But later, when Hitler received a telegraph from Hermann Göring, who had reached safety in the mountains, asking that he be allowed to take over the leadership of the Reich since Hitler had chosen to hole up in the bunker, he grew livid. In a terse reply, he said that Göring had committed "high treason." Bormann ordered the SS near Berghof to arrest Göring, which they did before dawn on April 25. Göring was immediately locked up.

The next day, April 26, Soviet artillery fire made the first direct hits on the Chancellery building and grounds, directly above the bunker. The bombardment was relentless, and it continued on April 27, fraying nerves even more. And then came the news that delivered the final blow to Hitler's composure: Himmler had asked to negotiate with the Allies and had even offered to surrender German armies in the west. According to eyewitnesses in the bunker, Hitler "raged like a madman" with a ferociousness no one had seen before. Himmler had been Hitler's most faithful servant since the start, a stalwart believer in the cause, but now the Nazi leader had no choice but to order his comrade's arrest. In a brutal act of instant revenge, Hitler instructed Himmler's personal representative in the bunker, Lieutenant General Hermann Fegelein, the husband of Eva Braun's sister, to leave the bunker and go outside to the Chancellery garden, where he was shot in the head. Fegelein had been seeking a way to escape to Sweden, as he wanted nothing to do with the suicide pact Hitler and Eva Braun had made if the Soviets ever got close to arresting them. After all this — the desertions of Göring and Himmler, the death of Fegelein, and the Soviets' imminent arrival in Berlin — it was time for Hitler to seriously plot his own death.

The night of April 28, Hitler dictated his last will and testament, in which he blamed the Jews, as usual, for everything that was wrong with the world, including all that had transpired during the war: "Above all I charge the leaders of the nation and those under them to scrupulous observance of the laws of race and to merciless opposition to the universal poisoner of all peoples, International Jewry. Before my death I expel the former Reichsführer-SS and Minister of the Interior Heinrich Himmler from the party and from all offices of State. In his stead I appoint Gauleiter Karl Hanke as Reichsführer-SS and Chief of the German Police, and Gauleiter Paul Giesler as Reichsminister of the interior. Göring and Himmler, quite apart from their disloyalty to my person, have done immeasurable harm to the country and the whole nation by secret negotiations with the enemy, which they have conducted without my knowledge and against my wishes, and by illegally attempting to seize power in the State for themselves." Just before midnight, Hitler married Eva Braun, after which he sipped champagne while reminiscing about better days gone by. In the end, Hitler admitted that death would be a welcome release for him after he had been so disappointed by his oldest friends.

With Soviet ground forces closing in on him from less than a mile away, Hitler accepted the inevitable. He took the final steps toward preparing for his death on April 29 by testing the potency of his poison on his favorite dog, Blondi, a German Shepherd, which died as a result. He then passed out poison capsules to his female secretaries while apologizing for the lack of a better going away present. He told them to swallow the pills the minute Soviets broke into the bunker so that they would not have to be humiliated.

At noon on April 30, Hitler convened the last meeting of his team, at which he was told the Soviets were only one block away. At 2 p.m., Hitler, a vegetarian, sat down and enjoyed his final meal: pasta and tomato sauce. He and his bride of less than 40 hours then bid a final farewell to Bormann, Goebbels, and the other remaining military aides and staff members. With Bormann and Goebbels remaining quietly close by, Hitler and Eva retreated to their private quarters. Soon, a gunshot rang out. At 3:30 p.m., Bormann and Goebbels went in and discovered Hitler's body sprawled out on the couch, blood pouring out of his head from a gunshot to his right temple. Eva Braun had died from swallowing a poison capsule. That evening, Hitler's young chef, Constanze Manziarly, was busy cooking fried eggs and mashed potatoes for Hitler, unaware that he was dead.

With Hitler out of the picture, the aides who remained began smoking ravenously — a practice Hitler had generally forbidden in his presence — while collectively trying to figure out how to escape Berlin without being captured by the Soviets. The next day, May 1, Goebbels and his wife poisoned their six children in the bunker, then went up to the garden and, at their own request, were shot in the back of the head by an SS man.

Before his death, Hitler named a successor — Karl Dönitz, the architect and commander of Hitler's submarine fleet and chief of the German Navy in the final stages of the war. After Hitler's suicide, Dönitz vowed outwardly to continue the struggle against the "Bolsheviks," but quietly opened negotiations to surrender to the enemy. Knowing that there was no way out for Germany, he authorized Colonel General Alfred Jodl to work out the terms of an unconditional surrender with the Allies.

News of Hitler's death was slow to reach the United States, and the reports that did finally trickle in were initially met with skepticism. Most American newspapers didn't run the news until May 2 — a full two days later — and even then, President Harry Truman was purposely cautious in confirming the reports at a press conference, couching his words with the catchphrase "to the best possible information." Newspapers around the world announced the death with bold, full-page headlines and, in some cases, with giddy delight. "Germans put out the news everyone hopes is true," the United Kingdom's *Daily Express* wrote. "Will rant no more," said Boston's *Daily Record*.

At 10:30 p.m. the day after the suicide, a German radio announcer somberly delivered the news that Hitler had died, fighting "at the head of his troops." He also told the world that Hitler's successor was Dönitz, who said "in the deepest sorrow and respect the German people bow." The radio announcement — coupled with the fact Hitler's remains were captured by the Soviets and subsequently locked behind the Iron Curtain for decades — proved fodder enough for conspiracy theorists, who wanted to make the case Hitler did not die in the bunker, but rather managed, somehow, to slip away like other high-ranking Nazi officials, including Adolf Eichmann and Josef Mengele, who skulked off to South America to live out their lives after Germany's collapse. Only in early 2018 did a study of Hitler's purported teeth in the Russian State Archive find them to be an exact match, confirming that Hitler did indeed die in his bunker, likely by taking cyanide and shooting himself in the head.

Folke felt very strongly there should be no misunderstanding: in no way did Hitler die a hero. He wrote: "It is true that he kept his leadership until the very last days of the Third Reich. But he had long before lost all capacity for taking any initiative. All he could do was to veto decisions made by his lieutenants. To his entourage he had become a figure of terror in almost the same degree as he was to the world at large. If anyone displeased him he immediately had an order for execution prepared. At this final stage, Adolf Hitler was physically and psychologically a branded man, in all probability marked by that disease which can offer an explanation for his insane acts and ideas. His hands shook, he could no longer walk, he could only cross the room with difficulty. He felt that the sands of his life were running out and was more than conscious of having failed completely, of his enemies being about to corner him, or the situation becoming more and more desperate. Until the last day he would telephone to Himmler, roaring out his accusations in a desperate attempt to conjure up a change in the situation."

Folke also wanted the German people to know what kind of men the leaders of the Third Reich really were. He said, "My experience tells me that they were men lacking in all moral conceptions, in all loftiness of mind. In the last act there they were, with their hideous pasts, desperately intriguing amongst themselves, while at the same time endeavoring to take shelter behind each other's backs, cowardly, undecided, irresolute. They were not fighting for an ideal, a belief, a conviction; they were fighting merely for their lives, which had been besmirched by crimes which could never be forgiven."

On April 28, Folke was waiting for word from Schellenberg regarding that fifth meeting with Himmler, when he turned on Radio Atlantic, a British propaganda service disguised as a free underground German station. Folke heard his name mentioned and knew instantly that the secret was out. The world would now know of his 78 days of negotiations with Himmler. As soon as Himmler got wind of the publicity, he angrily refused any further dealings. Folke and Schellenberg returned to Copenhagen on April 30 to check on how former prisoners were being treated. Events were moving quickly. Folke and Schellenberg worked to arrange the capitulation of the Germans in Norway, where a very determined group of Nazis resolved to fight to the death.

Finally, on May 7, Folke was back in Stockholm when he received word by phone that Germany had decided during the night on an unconditional surrender and that the capitulation would be signed. It was finally over. As he wrote, "the nightmare which the Nazi system signified had ceased to be a reality. Millions of people could now set their minds on the work of reconstruction, which was to recreate a happier world. The curtain now descended on a world which had seen a greater degree of evil and suffering than perhaps any earlier period in the history of Europe."

Himmler's downfall within the Reich came fast and furious. Dönitz initially thought about sending in specially trained guards to surround Himmler's quarters and hold him hostage. But then he reconsidered and instead requested a private meeting with Himmler. "I talked to Himmler alone in my room. I thought it wiser to keep my revolver hidden under a sheet of paper on my desk," Dönitz later wrote. "I gave him the telegram to read [naming Dönitz as Hitler's successor]. He grew pale. He pondered. Then he got up and congratulated me." Dönitz said that Himmler asked to serve as his second-in-command, a request that Dönitz immediately denied. Dönitz conceded that he wasn't able to discount Himmler completely, as much of the police force was still under his control.

But in the coming days, Himmler realized that his days in power were ending, as plea upon plea to fill various key positions were casually disregarded. He no longer had a place in the government of the country he loved so much. And so, on the morning of May 6, the man who had once been considered a candidate to succeed Hitler disappeared in a manner he had been secretly imagining for some time. He shaved off his mustache, donned a black eyepatch, put on the uniform of a rural policeman, and went out into the streets, pretending to be a simple German worker. The name on his fake credentials: Heinrich Hitzinger, a dead field policeman.

This unassuming little man could have easily blended into the countryside. But first, rather than trying to see his wife, he scurried off to be with his mistress and their two sons. He stayed with her, hiding out in her apartment, until he thought it safe to travel further. Finally, Heinrich Hitzinger moved south, to the Bremervorde British Army checkpoint, where two sentries were tasked with checking everyone's documents. If only he'd worn civilian clothes, he would have gotten away with it. But Heinrich was wearing a uniform, and the men were under strict orders to detain and carefully check out any and all Germans in uniform. They didn't really believe a rural policeman was anyone worth wasting time on, but they took his identity card and ordered him to come with them. This was merely routine — but Heinrich didn't know that. "It's no use," said Heinrich. He spoke no English and so was certain that the British sentries had recognized him. He was positive he was being arrested and he believed his life was over. "I am Reichsminister Heinrich Himmler," he told them proudly. He then demanded to be taken to see Eisenhower.

The sentries at first didn't believe him but, not willing to take any chances, they immediately notified their superiors, holding Himmler until they arrived. When Himmler's identity was verified, he was ordered to remove his German uniform so that he could be searched. Two cyanide vials were found and removed. When authorities offered Himmler a British uniform to wear, he refused, preferring instead to stand naked, with only a blanket to cover himself. Himmler was then transported to Lüneburg, where a sergeant major took him into a room being used for the processing of the area's Nazi leaders. Wanting to escape the gallows, Himmler removed the cyanide capsule he had been concealing in his teeth. As soon as his British captors heard a crunch coming from his mouth, they hoisted Himmler up by his legs while striking him on the back to make him cough up or throw up the poison. Their effort failed. Himmler briefly went into convulsions and slumped to the floor. Cyanide works fast.

Himmler died on May 23, 1945. Whatever his inflated ideas of his own importance, the Allies left his body in the room, covered only with a blanket, to rot over the coming days. In the words of the sergeant major who first brought him into the room, "I wrapped him up in a couple of blankets. Then I put two of our Army camouflage nets around him and tied him up with telephone wires. I had to dig his grave myself. Nobody will ever know where he is buried."

CHAPTER ELEVEN

The Beginning of a New Kind of Hell

On May 8, 1945, millions of people around the world celebrated Victory in Europe Day, rejoicing in the news that the Nazi war machine had finally been crushed. Elated victors poured into the streets, dancing and singing, hanging bunting and banners. In London, an estimated 50,000 people crammed into Piccadilly Circus to mark the triumph, despite still enduring rationing that had for years meant no bananas, very few eggs, and five inches of bath water per family once a week. The crowds were so enormous in New York's Times Square that 15,000 police officers had to be mobilized to control them.

Although victory in Japan wouldn't come until August 15, the war against Germany was finally over. It had cost the lives of so many. When the conflict began, the world's population was just over 2 billion. In less than a decade, the battle between the Axis and Allied powers had led to nearly 80 million deaths (including those from war-related diseases) — wiping out four percent of people on the planet. Two-thirds of the dead were civilians, and among them were six million Jews.

Peace brought its own set of complications, as devastated swaths of Europe and Asia were in dire need of rebuilding. Allied forces found themselves becoming occupiers, and an effort to permanently dismantle the military capabilities of once-great powers was launched. The challenges associated with a defeated Germany were so great that they prevented Americans from pulling back many of their forces in Europe and transferring them to the Far East.

For some, the end of the war meant the beginning of a different kind of hell. Europe was overwhelmed with "displaced persons" — a term coined in 1945 to describe the millions of refugees wandering the continent in search of a place to call home. Migration had, of course, occurred during the war, but the return of peace only led to a new surge of refugees, including released prisoners as well as citizens of occupied Axis powers. By some estimates, some 60 million Europeans became refugees over the course of the war. Lost or orphaned children were ubiquitous, with 300,000 in Yugoslavia alone. As late as 1951, a million people were still seeking a place to settle, according to the United Nations. The repatriation and resettlement of these displaced persons to their homelands required an urgent and Herculean effort.

Anticipating widespread devastation at the end of the war, in 1943 the Allies had established the United Nations Relief and Rehabilitation Administration (UNRRA) to provide assistance. And in 1945, after years of planning, the UN was created out of perceived necessity, as a means of doing a better job arbitrating international conflict than its predecessor, the League of Nations. The organization's impetus was the destruction caused by the war, but behind this lay a greater desire to prevent this kind of global battle from ever happening again.

The war spawned many mini — and a few not-so-mini — postwar wars. Perhaps the most complex of these would be the 1948 war in Palestine, the conflict that led to the creation of the state of Israel for Jews and the al-Nakba (The Catastrophe) for Palestinians. Jews fleeing persecution in Europe wanted to establish a safe haven in what was then an Arab- and Muslim-majority territory in the Ottoman and later British Empire. But Arabs saw the land as rightfully theirs. Although both Jews and Arabs date their claims to the land back a couple thousand years, the current ongoing conflict began at the end of the 19th century.

On November 2, 1917, British Foreign Secretary Arthur James Balfour had submitted a public statement of intent to create a "national home" for the Jewish people in Palestine — the Balfour Declaration. Arab reactions to the announcement were far from favorable. The declaration meant that Palestine would fall under British occupation, and Palestinians would not gain their independence. Plus, at the time, Jews only made up 10 percent of the population; some 90 percent of the population of Palestine were Arab Muslims and Christians. The 1917 declaration referred to this overwhelming Palestinian majority as simply "existing non-Jewish communities," with "civil and religious rights," but not political ones.

Folke emerged from the Second World War fairly anonymously — most people were unaware of the scope of the part he had played. And his feats might nearly have vanished into historical oblivion if not for a small memoir he wrote within a few short weeks about his experiences negotiating with Himmler. The book was called *The Curtain Falls*, and it became a runaway best seller, translated into more than a dozen languages. From that point on, Folke's name was entwined with any description of the final weeks of war. The book turned the aristocrat into something of a celebrity. The fact that he was the first non-Nazi to sit across a conference table from one of history's most vile monsters was a true tale of intrigue and heroism. The public ate it up.

As word seeped out of Folke's accomplishments, the accolades poured in. There were honorary doctorate degrees from both Uppsala University in Sweden and Copenhagen University. France conferred upon him the Grand Cross of the Legion of Honour, the highest civilian decoration in that country, and the World Jewish Congress awarded him a citation. On a more personal level, he received a plethora of gifts, including many beautifully embroidered dolls from liberated women, rebuilding their lives in various parts of the world.

But perhaps the most satisfying distinction came in November 1945, when Folke was promoted from vice-chairman to chairman of the Swedish Red Cross in succession to his 84-year-old uncle, Prince Carl. Folke had big shoes to fill. When Carl became chairman in 1906, , the membership numbered 4,500. When he left his post as leader, the membership had ballooned to 550,000. This was a time when the International Red Cross was enjoying a lot of attention, having been awarded the 1944 Nobel Peace Prize for its services to prisoners of war and relief work in occupied countries.

But even as Folke's work was being rewarded, accusations were being hurled at him too. Some critics maintained he hadn't done enough to save Jews from the concentration camps and had focused too much on Scandinavian prisoners; others downplayed his role in the rescue operation. And then there was the touchy matter of the Bernadottes having hosted Walter Schellenberg in their own home in May 1945, during the final weeks of the war. Folke got along well with Schellenberg and felt he owed the Nazi for the success he achieved with Himmler. And yet even Estelle believed the move was a serious lapse in judgement. Folke Bernadotte Jr. still remembers the "excitement" of having a "real Nazi" staying with the family. "Schellenberg was a nasty Nazi but a very nice man," he said. "When he was in our home, the study door would be closed. Everything going on seemed to be very secret." After the war, Bernadotte vouched for Schellenberg's character at the Nuremberg Trials. Schellenberg, who testified against other SS officers, was sentenced to six years in prison. But he was released early due to a worsening liver condition, and he died in Turin, Italy, in 1952.

At least outwardly, Folke appeared unfazed by the criticism. He plunged into postwar humanitarian efforts the same way he had the White Bus rescue mission. And much of that work had to do with helping Germans, particularly German children, who faced death if they did not receive aid.

From 1945 to 1948, Folke transformed from a talented but amateur statesman to a widely respected and well-known public servant of the highest integrity. His military experience helped set him up for his new role, having instilled in him the value of discipline and dedication. He had become even more adept at listening and formulating opinions that incorporated as many people's good ideas as possible. In fact, for the first time since he left the army, he held a real and permanent position of authority, one that required him to formulate policy and oversee a large staff.

His responsibilities fell into three categories: international relief, domestic Red Cross work, and International Red Cross politics. Since the colossal UNRRA and its affiliated organizations were in charge of the bulk of relief efforts in Western Europe after the war, Sweden's sphere of relief wound up encompassing Germany and Soviet-dominated countries. Folke was fine with this arrangement, especially since Sweden had not yet joined the United Nations. To Folke, Nazism had been an abomination, but he sympathized with the German people, who in his opinion were also Hitler's victims. Folke was horrified by the decimation of German cities, which had left millions homeless. The entire country was in chaos, and there wasn't enough food to go around.

But in the Allied camp, many would continue to harbor animosities toward the Germans. They wondered why Germany should be given assistance when so many other countries were experiencing shortages of the most basic commodities. But unlike Japan or the Soviet Union, Germany had no national government until 1949. No central authority was available to help cities to rebuild. Even so, the only real relief effort many authorities could get on board with was one restricted to helping children under the age of 12. Folke spent the first few months after the war arguing against collective punishment, a tool the Nazis had used to demoralize civilian populations in occupied Europe. But it was a losing battle.

In addition to helping Germany, Folke also tried to broaden the scope of his Red Cross contacts in countries within the Russian sphere of influence. As the war moved into its final stages, suspicions that would eventually fuel the Cold War were already festering between the United States and the Soviet Union. The destructive capabilities of the atomic bomb, which the United States dropped on Japan in August 1945, made the Soviets justifiably nervous. The United States also provoked the ire of Russia when it abruptly cut off all military and financial aid to the Soviet Union upon the war's end, right at the moment when Russian citizens most needed the help.

For its part, the Soviet Union was sending clear signals it had no intention of giving up the territory it had gained from the Nazis or of allowing an honest election in a conquered Poland, as previously promised — Joseph Stalin knew that would only result in an anti-Soviet government. Folke believed that if the Soviet Union wasn't challenged in Eastern Europe, another war would soon follow. If he did harbor any glimmer of optimism, it was pinned on the hope that Stalin might learn from Hitler's mistakes and pull back the Iron Curtain. That, of course, wasn't to be the case.

Folke's first humanitarian foray immediately after VE-Day was to fly to northern Norway to check on the status of Russian prisoners of war there. When liberation came in 1945, about 84,000 Soviets were on Norwegian soil, many of them held in remote areas within the Arctic Circle, in the most inhospitable conditions imaginable. Most had been forced into labor, building roads and railways with little nourishment. In June 1945, the Swedish Red Cross moved in to provide food and medical treatment to the prisoners, who needed to regain their strength if they were ever to repair their lives following repatriation.

Behind the scenes, Folke diligently tried to convince the Soviet authorities that these Russians should be allowed to return home. But Stalin thought of any Soviet who fell into German hands as a traitor and no longer worthy of government protection. Russia also didn't want to take back anyone who might have gotten a feel for Western civilization and could undermine the general public's illusion that Russia was some kind of workers' paradise. Anyone touched by the West, it seemed, was forevermore a pariah in the eyes of his or her countrymen. Even so, from 1943 until early 1947, western countries, led by Britain and the United States, returned nearly 2.5 million prisoners of war and refugees to the Soviet Union, with little regard for their individual wishes and genuine fears — or the fact that many faced treason trials and execution immediately after stepping foot in their home country.

Folke also negotiated and operated relief projects in communist countries and established contacts with no fewer than eight communist governments, to which he offered help with youth, medical, and educational projects. He helped establish at least a dozen successful aid efforts in Poland, Hungary, Romania, Yugoslavia, Czechoslovakia, and Albania. In Poland, for example, a large center for destitute Polish children had been set up with the help of the Swedish Red Cross. Poland had been devastated by the Nazis during the war and now was under staunch Soviet control. By the time Folke visited the center in 1946, 2,400 children had been fed, nursed, and educated in the previous 12 months. Folke also traveled to Romania, occupied by Soviet troops in 1944, to ensure the food and clothing that Sweden had sent as relief were reaching their intended target — the starving millions. Everywhere he went, Russian authorities tried to prevent him from freely traveling around. The Russians were skeptical about relief work, and this skepticism seeped into the communization of the Red Cross organizations in the countries the Soviets controlled. Folke was aghast that some Romanian officials believed rumors that the Americans were using relief supplies as a cover for smuggling arms into Romania to supply an anti-communist uprising.

In the fall of 1947, Folke later wrote, it was clear Russia had parted company with western Allies. Prominent on the agenda of a regional conference of European Red Cross agencies organized by the Yugoslavian Red Cross in Belgrade was a discussion of the operation of relief programs in various countries. The Russian delegate, supported by representatives of several Eastern European countries, took to the floor to lambaste "so-called" supervisors from aid organizations abroad and to demand they return home immediately. Their presence, he claimed, was an infringement on the sovereignty of the countries receiving aid and proof that some places were receiving preferential treatment at the expense of others. The Russians were putting on a dangerous show, flexing their muscles while doling out lies. According to Folke, Red Cross relief work was carried out with no regard to race, creed, or political affiliation. Much to the dismay of the Allies, the nations of Albania, Bulgaria, Czechoslovakia, Hungary, Poland, Romania, and Yugoslavia would all have communist governments by 1948.

In Germany, Folke's aid efforts were dependent on a chain of daily soup kitchens set up in the four military sectors of Berlin — all of which suffered major food shortages — and later in other cities, including Hamburg, where the people endured an even more dreary and meager existence. On July 28, 1943, a British bombing raid on Hamburg — during which 2,326 tons of bombs were dropped in just 43 minutes — killed 42,000 German civilians and created a firestorm that scorched eight square miles. The war had left everyone in dire straits. That's why Folke paid so many visits to Hamburg, where almost every shop was empty; even if you had money, there was nothing to buy. The only currency that carried any weight was cigarettes. Everywhere he looked, people begged in the streets and orphans wandered aimlessly. Thievery was relentless. To help the community, the so-called "Big Kitchen," or the place where soup was prepared for the German children, was established there.

Folke toured the facility and found the operation to be nothing if not efficient. At 5:30 a.m. sharp, the cooks got to work making soup. Between 8:30 and 9:30, containers were filled and then delivered on big trucks to various canteens. According to Folke, at first mothers were given the soup to bring to their children, but the children were soon required to show up in person and eat their soup on-site. The mothers protested: accompanying their children wasted time they desperately needed to scrape together their families' subsistence. But this was the only way to control the distribution and ensure the soup really was benefiting those under 12. Feeding German children was a colossal undertaking, and Folke was proud of its success. By July 1, 1948, about 67 million meals would be distributed, saving countless lives.

The nature of the relief effort began to change markedly in June 1947. In a speech to the graduating class of Harvard University, U.S. Secretary of State George Marshall issued a call for a comprehensive program to rebuild Europe. Fearing communist expansion amid the rapid deterioration of European economies, Congress passed the Economic Cooperation Act in March 1948 and approved funding that would eventually rise to more than $12 billion for the rebuilding of Western Europe.

As the direction of Europe's recovery started to shift, Folke's relief work in Germany and elsewhere in Europe began to sputter. So he turned his attention to Greece and Turkey, two places he visited in late April 1948 at the invitation of the national leaders, who welcomed any and all help with relief efforts. He was about to leave to do a survey of the region when, much to his surprise, a telegram arrived. He read it, but hardly understood what it said.

The telegram was from New York, from the United Nations, inviting him to serve as the body's first mediator in Palestine. Folke couldn't quite believe it. Not only had he not applied for the job, he didn't even know such a position was available. But the opportunity was enticing.

Although Folke's humanitarian efforts were still important to him, the UN assignment would give him a more auspicious role on the world stage. In many ways, it was just the challenge he needed. His private life had grown so routine it was almost monotonous. The regular family trips to the Swedish coast in summer and to New York at Christmas were pleasant enough, but Folke yearned to broaden his horizons. Financially, the Bernadottes were set for life, as Estelle's wealthy father had already handed over her share of the inheritance. Folke never received, nor did he need, a regular salary from the Red Cross.

But why did the United Nations want him as mediator between the Jews and Arabs in a hostile conflict he knew nothing about? Folke was the first to admit that his "knowledge of the situation in Palestine was very superficial." And yet there were many reasons he was the fledgling agency's top pick. By the end of the Second World War, a 50-year-old Folke had built a reputation for not only being a shrewd negotiator, but also for being able to stay cool under pressure and to act decisively even with limited information. Also working in his favor were his citizenship of a neutral nation and his friendship with former colleague Trygve Lie, the Norwegian politician who, in 1946, became the first secretary-general of the United Nations.

Before accepting the post, Folke sought the counsel of his wife. "We knew that the task was one of enormous size and might possibly prove completely insoluble," Folke said. "We argued this way, that if, in the event of my being definitely offered the post, I were to refuse it, I should probably reproach myself for the rest of my life because I had not even tried to make any contribution toward clearing up this difficult situation." Estelle said later, "He decided that he probably had one chance in a hundred to succeed, but accepted on the possibility of that one chance." Even so, many friends tried to talk him out of taking the post. Folke

Bernadotte Jr. recalled, "His friends warned him that this was no scout camp."

"Perhaps it was an advantage that I had not concerned myself with the Palestine question before. There was always a slight chance that an outsider might contribute new points of view toward the problem," Folke later wrote. "But I gladly admitted that the conscientious work done by countless commissions in respect to this question argued against such a possibility. That I finally decided to accept was mainly due to the fact that, because of the serious character of the problem, I did not feel that I had the right to husband my strength."

On May 20, 1948, he accepted the role just six days after the establishment of the state of Israel. His principal supporters were the United States and Britain. Folke's ultimate responsibility, as outlined in a General Assembly resolution on May 14, was to "promote a peaceful adjustment of the future situation of Palestine."

For the rookie United Nations, Folke's mediation was aimed at nothing less than finding a solution for its first real diplomatic quandary — a conflict that dated back to the end of the 19th century. "We have tried for years to solve the problem," British envoy Sir Alexander Cadogan told the General Assembly delegates in March 1947. "Having failed so far, we now bring the Palestine question to the United Nations, in the hope that it can succeed where we have not." Drained financially and emotionally after the Second World War, Britain couldn't wait to hand the troublesome territory over to the UN. The UN felt it had a clear mandate and full constitutional authority to restore order within Palestine and to stave off intervention from outsiders.

It's important to understand the quagmire Folke found himself in. On November 29, 1947, the United Nations General Assembly had adopted a resolution to partition Britain's former Palestinian mandate between Arabs and Jews, laying the groundwork for the formation of the Jewish state of Israel in May 1948. The plan, which organized Palestine into three Jewish sections, four Arab sections, and the internationally administered city of Jerusalem, was supported by Western nations as well as the Soviet Union but was strongly opposed by Arab nations. The war-weary British paid little heed to the turmoil building in the weeks leading up to their withdrawal. They just wanted out. In the book, *The Seat of Pilate*, John Marlowe wrote of the inauspicious final few moments of British rule, "The Union Jack was lowered and with the speed of an execution and the silence of a ship that passes in the night British rule in Palestine came to an end." President Harry S. Truman recognized Israel as a legitimate state just 11 minutes after its founding, making the United States the first country to do so. A few minutes later, the Soviet Union followed suit.

The Arabs were opposed to the resolution's terms, which granted 55 percent of the land to the Jews, even though they constituted only 33 percent of the population. They were also against the idea of having no choice but to remain in Jewish territory. The resolution didn't sit well with the Jews either, as they envisaged Jerusalem as Israel's capital. Menachem Begin, leader of the Zionist terrorist group the Irgun, and a future premier of Israel, declared, "The partition of Palestine is illegal. It will never be recognized . . . Jerusalem was and will forever be our capital, and Eretz Israel [the biblical land of Israel which included all of Mandatory Palestine] will be restored to the people of Israel. All of it. And forever." The United States tried to find some middle ground by backing the United Nations resolution, while also urging the Arabs and Jews to continue to talk. But within days of its passage, the UN resolution sparked violent clashes between Palestinians and Jews throughout the region, fanning the flames of the Arab-Israeli conflict that continues to this day.

Through the following month, when British rule formally came to an end and Israel declared its independence on May 14, civil war raged in Palestine. On paper and on the ground, the Palestinians had every advantage. Not only were there twice as many of them, but they also occupied the territory at higher altitudes and enjoyed the support of the sympathetic regimes around them. The Arabs got off to a good start when, on the eve of May 14, they launched an air attack on Tel Aviv. But the Israelis didn't back down; they resisted hard. An invasion of Arab armies from Iraq, Syria, Egypt, Lebanon, and Saudi Arabia followed. The Israelis resisted again. As isolated and outnumbered as they were, the Jews were far better organized, motivated, financed, equipped, and trained than their adversaries — and they also enjoyed the support of Britain and the United States. Their opponents, meanwhile, were so fragmented — by geography, tradition, and history — that the term "Palestinian" was rendered nearly meaningless. The Jews soon got the upper hand, and the Palestinian refugee crisis was born, with hundreds of thousands of Palestinian Arabs choosing — or being forced — to evacuate their homes. Resentments mushroomed on both sides.

For Folke, trying to forge peace among parties with claims to the land going back centuries would be like trying to build a castle with a sand shovel.

Folke, however, was undeterred. At his disposal was an assistant — André-Pierre Sérot, a French air force colonel — and 100 unarmed French military personnel who could act as a UN truce observer team. Ralph Bunche, a senior UN official and scholar, was also asked to assist Folke, and the two held an inaugural meeting in Paris. In no time, Folke won Bunche over with his affability, command of English, and determination to succeed where others had failed. "I think," Bunche wrote, "we shall get on well, for he seems to be a man who will listen seriously to advice." Even though they could not have been more different, the two formed an immediate bond.

Raised in Detroit, Bunche was an African-American whose grandmother had been born into slavery. As a young man, Bunche sold newspapers and took any odd job he could find in order to contribute to his hard-pressed family's finances. Folke, of course, grew up in a royal family that never wanted for anything. But the two got along spectacularly well and shared a strong desire to bring peace to Palestine. Bunche described Folke in his diary like this: "The Count is affable, speaks good English, is fairly tall, slender, with a deep-lined face, but nice looking . . . He is eager to get to work. He emphasizes frankness and punctuality. He says that if he advances an idea he relishes criticism provided it is accompanied by an alternative plan."

While his intentions may have been noble, the result was a mediation mission doomed before it even began. Folke wasn't trusted by the Israelis, who were infuriated by stories that he had played nice with the Nazis. There was also, of course, the lingering criticism in some circles that Folke had ignored the Jews when rescuing people from the concentration camps, even though the World Jewish Congress estimated that many thousands of Jewish lives were saved by the White Buses. And he offended the Jews again when he decided to make his first stop as mediator in Cairo. "It was the Arabs after all who were adopting the offensive," Folke explained. "It was consequently with them we ought to seek contact first in any question of truce or ceasefire." But to the Israelis, there was no reason for him to meet with those they believed had openly defied the UN.

While Folke was in Cairo, a good omen emerged: the UN Security Council adopted a British resolution that called on all parties to lay down their weapons for four weeks, which would create a space for mediation to occur. But when Folke met with Israel's founding prime minister, David Ben-Gurion, for the first time after arriving in Israel, he got a frosty reception. Ben-Gurion opposed any resolution that appeared to treat both sides as equal partners since, in his mind, the Arabs were nothing but law-breaking aggressors. Folke spent the next several days crisscrossing the region, haggling with both parties in an attempt to find mutuality amid the contempt. His travels and powers of persuasion paid off when, at noon on June 9, the governments of Egypt, Lebanon, Syria, and Saudi Arabia announced they would accept a four-week truce in Palestine starting at 6 a.m. on June 11. Two hours later, Transjordan did the same, followed by a reluctant Israel. The agreement called for a ban on "all acts of armed force in Palestine for a period of four weeks" as well as "relief to populations of both sides in municipal areas which have suffered severely from the conflicts, as in Jerusalem and Jaffa . . . administered by the International Red Cross . . . to ensure that reserve stocks of essential supplies shall not be substantially greater or less at the end of the truce than they are at the beginning." Bunche later called the truce the result of "the most intensive diplomatic negotiation that has ever been undertaken in the history of diplomacy."

But the conditions Folke placed on the truce to curb arms and immigration, which hampered Israeli's ability to build an army, riled the hardline Sternists. Named after Avraham Stern — who was shot and killed in February 1942 after masterminding a wave of terrorist attacks on British targets — the Sternists' goal had always been securing Jewish independence at any cost. Ben-Gurion, too, was suspicious of the Swede. He asked his cabinet, "Why does Bernadotte think we have to trust him? Did we choose him? And why is he preparing his final draft [of the truce proposal] in Egypt?" Although both sides accepted Folke's conditions on paper, in the end neither fully respected the truce and both found ways to skirt the restrictions. The Israelis and Arabs used the time to fortify their positions, a direct violation of the ceasefire's terms. In the end, the shaky truce held together — but only by a thread.

Even so, the ceasefire gave Folke the cover he needed to put forward his first proposal in an effort to get a conversation started that might lead to a lasting peace. It was June 28, barely a month since he had taken on his new assignment. The Bernadotte Plan would divide Palestine into two states, one Jewish and one Arab. They would form an economic union, but each state would retain control over its own affairs. Jerusalem would belong to the Arab part of the union, with a local self-government for the Jewish population.

Although the plan drew a harsh response from both camps, the Zionists singled out one paragraph in particular as unacceptable: "It is, however, undeniable that no settlement can be just and complete if recognition is not accorded to the rights of the Arab refugee to return to the home from which he has been dislodged by the hazards and strategy of the armed conflict between Arabs and Jews in Palestine. . . . It would be an offense against the principles of elemental justice if these innocent victims of the conflict were denied the right to return to their homes while Jewish immigrants flow into Palestine and indeed, at least offer the threat of permanent replacement of the Arab refugees who have been rooted in the land for centuries."

As soon as the ceasefire formally expired on July 9, hostilities spiraled out of control — yet again — and the initiative collapsed. In September, Folke put forth a second plan: a two-state solution that abandoned the idea of an economic union. The new road map called for Jerusalem to remain under UN protection and recognized the right of return for Palestinians. If returning was impossible, compensation would be paid. The second plan was similar to the first one, except that it allowed for an independent Jewish state, albeit a small one, and the internationalization of Jerusalem.

The plan was seen by many Jews as pro-Arab, with the issue of refugees particularly hard to stomach. The Jewish state would have covered only some 20 percent of Palestine.

The Jews thought it clear that Folke had a soft spot for the Palestinian refugees and that he'd do anything to protect their interests. If he was given the chance to argue the case before the UN General Assembly, Israel's very existence might be at stake. And Israel might never have the chance to achieve its goal of controlling both banks of the Jordan River. One way or another, some felt, the aristocratic mediator had to go.

With this second proposal on the table and about to be reviewed and discussed by both sides, Folke made his way to Jerusalem — and straight into an ambush.

CHAPTER TWELVE

A Heart-Wrenching Sorrow

It was five p.m. on September 17, 1948. Sitting in the back seat of a new Chrysler, Folke had finally begun to unwind. The last few days had been something of a whirlwind, long and hectic and draining.

The morning prior, Folke had flown into Beirut, already looking tired as he emerged from the aircraft. He confided to the officials there to greet him that he was happy to be alive: A radio station on the Greek island of Rhodes had picked up a false report that a policeman had found Folke murdered on a street there. In Beirut, he submitted a final report on the truce respecting Palestine that had been in place from June 11 to July 9; his report noted that, in light of a laundry list of handicaps, "the shortage of observers, the impossibility of advance preparation, the inability to establish the battle lines as of June 11, the lack of means of transport and telecommunications — the surprising feature of the truce supervision is not that it had shortcomings but that it worked as well as it did in practice."

The Beirut stopover also was key because of the refugee situation, as the city was to serve as the headquarters of the relief mission. Before long, ships would be moving in and out of the port on the city's northern Mediterranean coast, a crossroads for eastern and western civilizations, from the 50 or so countries and organizations that had promised food, tents, medical supplies, and other assistance. These items would then be parceled out to the various refugee camps set up in Syria, Lebanon, Transjordan, and elsewhere.

A clause making sure the refugees were cared for had been conspicuous in Folke's first peace plan, and it remained significant in his second. On August 7, Folke estimated there were 300,000 to 400,000 Palestinian refugees, many of whom had fled at the first whiff of grapeshot, leaving everything they owned behind. Folke described their living conditions — with no food, water, shelter, medicine — as "appalling." The U.S. State Department reported similar numbers to President Truman on August 19, noting that a refugee's average daily ration, made up entirely by bread, constituted no more than 600 calories. Relief was urgently needed to prevent the large-scale tragedy bound to occur once the rainy season started and winter set in.

To Folke, the crux of the clash between the two sides was whether the refugees would eventually be allowed by Israel to return to their homes. "In this connection," according to Jefferson Patterson, the U.S. charge d'affaires in Cairo, "Bernadotte said PGI [Provisional Government of Israel] was 'showing signs of swell-head.' In regard to the property of Arab refugees . . . [Folke] said apparently most had been seized for use by Jews." Israeli officials insisted the refugees were not their responsibility, claiming that everything possible was done to prevent an exodus, "which was a direct result of the folly of the Arab states in organizing and launching a war of aggression against Israel." And even if they wanted to, officials could not admit Arab refugees as they would constitute a fifth column — a subversive group sympathetic to Israel's enemies. Like Folke, Dean Rusk, director of the Office of UN Affairs, as well as other U.S. officials, all agreed that, contrary to what Israelis believed, the refugees posed no security risk to Israel. When Folke confronted the Israeli Foreign Minister Moshe Sharett with the need to take them in, he was told that, economically, there also was simply no room for the Arabs since their space was needed by Jewish immigrants.

With rising tensions threatening to destabilize an already imperfect peace even further, Folke flew into Kalandia, an Arab civilian airport north of Jerusalem, the following morning, on September 17, aboard a white DC-3 bearing the symbol of the International Red Cross. As the plane started its descent, word came from Haifa — the northern Israeli port city — that all aircraft landing at Kalandia should expect to be fired on. But Folke and the others paid little heed to the warning, which they considered an Israeli scare tactic. The plane landed safely.

Before the team set off, Age Lundström, Folke's personal representative and chief of staff, relayed another ominous rumor: every other vehicle should expect to be fired on at the Mandelbaum Gate, a concrete and barbed wire checkpoint between the Israeli and Jordanian sectors of Jerusalem. Lundström asked Folke if it might not be wiser to proceed from Ramallah via Latrun to Jerusalem. This circuitous route was undoubtedly safer but would take at least an hour longer to complete. Folke answered, "I would not do that. I have to take the same risks as my observers, and moreover, I think no one has the right to refuse me permission to pass through the lines. If I do not go, I will be admitting that they have the right to prevent me from crossing the lines."

Folke's entire visit to Jerusalem was choreographed to serve as an example to the truce observers. In Folke's opinion, any hesitation to visit the same dangerous hotspots the observers had fanned out over to do their work would send the wrong message. Why should he accept any form of protection that wasn't also available to the observers? He knew it was risky. Recently, the observers had been unnerved by an uptick in sniper activity, and some had been held up by the gangs of outlaws that infested the outskirts of the city. But Folke would have it no other way.

During a visit to the Palestinian city of Ramallah, a bullet struck one of the armored cars in Folke's convoy, proving that nothing could guarantee the mediator's safety. No one was hurt and, according to army liaison officer Moshe Hillman, Folke was even a little bit proud of the bullet hole, noting to his fellow travelers that the UN flag was something of a rabbit's foot. Inspecting the damage outside the Rockefeller Museum in Jerusalem shortly afterward, he admitted, "I do not like irregulars and I do not like being shot at." As he drove off, a newspaper reporter shouted, "Good luck." Folke answered, "I'll need it."

From the very beginning of his tenure as mediator, Folke had realized the Israelis considered him partial and were going to treat him as an enemy. Lehi placards posted throughout Jerusalem demanded he leave the country and remove the international presence impeding Jewish control of the city. "Stockholm is yours. Jerusalem is ours. You work in vain," they said. Folke considered Lehi demands the desperate chatter of extremists. He had never given a lot of heed to the threats against his life.

But already in July, two Sternists had told *New York Times* columnist C.L. Sulzberger that "we intend to kill Bernadotte and any other uniformed United Nations observers who come to Jerusalem." Asked why, they replied that their organization was determined to seize all of Jerusalem for the state of Israel and would block any interference.

The Israeli government, too, had been critical of Folke's participation in the negotiations from the start. On July 1, 1948, Folke put out a statement that the Arab nations were reluctant to resume fighting in Palestine and that the conflict now consisted of "incidents." A spokesman for the Israeli government replied, "Count Bernadotte has described the renewed Arab attacks as 'incidents.' When human lives are lost, when the truce is flagrantly violated . . . it shows a lack of sensitivity to describe all these as incidents, or to suggest as Count Bernadotte does, that the Arabs had some reason for saying no. . . . Such an apology for aggression does not augur well for any successful resumption by the mediator of his mission." A report in the *New York Herald Tribune* on July 7, 1948, quoted a highly placed Israeli government official as saying that any suggestion of Arab control over Jerusalem "destroyed any possibility of concessions on our part in regard to the rest of the plan. Psychologically, it was a grave error. Bernadotte failed to understand that most Jews would rather give up Tel Aviv or any other city rather than let the Arabs take Jerusalem."

In Jerusalem, Folke and his party were to meet with UN truce observers and inspect several proposed sites for their new headquarters. Weeks earlier, he and his staff had set up shop, temporarily, in the Hotel des Roses on Rhodes, but Folke felt the location was too far removed from the action and from the people he needed to be near. He also naively believed his presence in Jerusalem might damp down the deep mistrust and tensions that continued to build on both sides. After visiting several possible spots, Folke was due to discuss the issue at 4:30 p.m. with Dov Joseph, military governor of the New City of Jerusalem, outside the old city walls.

That appointment was rescheduled to 6:30 p.m., giving Folke time to visit the Jerusalem Agricultural School, where he picked up French UN observer and decorated war hero André-Pierre Sérot who — at the last minute — asked to be seated next to Folke in the Chrysler. He wanted to personally thank him for rescuing his wife, who had spent the war in the Dachau concentration camp and, according to Sérot, owed her life to Folke. Folke's car was the last in a three-car convoy that then proceeded on to the YMCA to pick up a copy of the truce regulations so that Folke could take it to the meeting with Joseph. Each car clearly displayed UN flags and Red Cross banners. No one in the convoy was armed, and Folke repeatedly refused to wear a flak jacket. The vehicles traveled toward Joseph's house in the Jerusalem neighborhood of Rehavia, eventually starting their final ascent of a narrow road through the Katamon Quarter, which was under Israeli army control and largely deserted.

No one in the first car, a DeSoto, least of all the Israeli captain assigned to escort the VIPs, seemed overly alarmed when a new-looking Israeli Army jeep veered in front of them and came to a stop, blocking their path. They assumed it was just another improvised checkpoint. Fingers on triggers, three soldiers approached the DeSoto in khaki shorts and berets — typical Israeli Army attire. The three young Swedes and a Belgian in the passenger seats cast about for their papers. "It's okay, boys," the Israeli officer explained. "Let us pass. It's the UN mediator."

In an instant, one of the three men ran over to the Chrysler, confirmed it was Folke in the back seat, and thrust the barrel of his German-made MP 40 submachine gun through the open rear window. At point-blank range, he pumped six bullets into Folke, including one to his heart, and another 17 bullets into the head and chest of Sérot. The Israeli captain, Moshe Hillman, rushed from the first car to the Chrysler. Sickened at the sight of the widening pools of blood forming around the two men's bodies, he chanted, "My God, oh my God," before jumping in beside the driver, a UN security man recruited from the FBI, and ordering him to drive as fast as he could to the Hadassah hospital, only a short distance away.

Major General Age Lundström, head of UN Truce Supervision in Palestine and Folke's personal representative, was in the same vehicle as Folke. He described the attack like this: "In the Katamon quarter, we were held up by a Jewish Army type jeep placed in a roadblock and filled with men in

Jewish Army uniforms. At the same moment, I saw an armed man coming from this jeep. I took little notice of this because I merely thought it was another checkpoint. However, he put a Tommy gun through the open window on my side of the car, and fired point blank at Count Bernadotte and Colonel Sérot. I also heard shots fired from other points, and there was considerable confusion. . . . Colonel Sérot fell in the seat in back of me, and I saw at once that he was dead. Count Bernadotte bent forward, and I thought at the time he was trying to get cover. I asked him, 'Are you wounded?' He nodded, and fell back. . . . When we arrived [at the Hadassah hospital] . . . I carried the Count inside and laid him on the bed . . . I took off the Count's jacket and tore away his shirt and undervest. I saw that he was wounded around the heart and that there was also a considerable quantity of blood on his clothes about it. When the doctor arrived, I asked if anything could be done, but he replied that it was too late." The 53-year-old UN mediator officially charged with bringing peace to a Holy Land at war, and his chief UN observer, Sérot, were both dead.

Members of Lohamei Herut Israel, or Fighters for the Freedom of Israel (Lehi) — better known as the Stern Gang — had solicited information about Folke's schedule from sympathetic journalists, which is how they knew about the last-minute change in the timing of Folke's meeting with Dov Joseph. Lehi saw Folke as nothing but a stooge of the British and their Arab allies, someone who had broken bread with the Nazis, and who therefore could never be trusted. Lehi leaders feared that Israeli leadership would agree to Folke's peace proposals, which they regarded as calamitous, and Lehi had decided a week earlier to have Folke killed.

What they didn't know was that the Israeli leaders had already secretly decided to reject his plan. Also unknown to the wider population: Folke's new proposal dropped the idea of turning over Jerusalem to Jordan and instead reverted to the partition plan's designation of it as an international city. The gunmen cut down Folke without knowing he no longer advocated handing Jerusalem over to the Arabs.

As the car carrying Folke and Sérot raced to the hospital, the Lehi assassins escaped to the nearby religious community of Sha'arei Pina, where they hid with Lehi sympathizers for a few days before absconding to Tel Aviv in the back of a furniture truck. Fleeing the scene of the assassination, one of the killers had dropped the detachable barrel and magazine from his weapon, which allowed investigators to determine its type.

The next day, headlines in newspapers around the world proclaimed the news: "Folke Bernadotte Murdered During Freedom Mission to Israel." Flags in cities from Haifa to Stockholm were flown at half-mast. The United Nations Security Council condemned the killings as "a cowardly act which appears to have been committed by a criminal group of terrorists in Jerusalem while the United Nations representative was fulfilling his peace-seeking mission in the Holy Land."

The assassination also drew an official condemnation from the Israeli government, and a promise of a full investigation and speedy arrests. A group calling itself "The Fatherland Front" claimed responsibility for the murders, but most everyone knew that it was only a cover name for Lehi designed to deflect reprisals against the group. The assassins didn't realize it was Sérot next to Folke — they thought it was Lundström, whom they also intended to murder but who escaped injury. In a printed statement acknowledging responsibility for the assassinations, the killers apologized for murdering Sérot "by mistake." Lehi was under intense international scrutiny and condemnation, with the Israeli government making a show of arresting many of its members and forcibly disarming others. No one was charged with the murders, however, nor was there even an outcry against the killings among Israelis.

Two Lehi leaders, Nathan Yellin-Mor and Matityahu Shmuelevitz, were found guilty of belonging to a terrorist organization and sentenced by a military court to prison terms of eight years and five years respectively. But then they were immediately pardoned and released as part of a "general" amnesty. They had won over the court with their promises to be law-abiding citizens. Yitzhak Shamir was not only implicated but in fact identified as a mastermind of the murders. He was never tried, however, and went on to become prime minister in 1983. He served two terms.

Israel's obvious reluctance to make the assassins pay for their crimes resulted in the first UN Security Council criticism of the fledgling country. On October 19, 1948, the council unanimously passed a resolution expressing its "concern" that Israel had "to date submitted no report to the Security Council or the Acting Mediator regarding the progress of the investigation into the assassination." An official inquiry by Sweden produced a report in 1950 that expressed its dissatisfaction that Israel had made no progress in the hunt for the killers, charging Israel's investigation had been so negligent that "doubt must exist as to whether the Israeli authorities really tried to bring the inquiry to a positive result." Even Israel later came to the same conclusion, conceding that there were major shortcomings in its own investigation. Ultimately, in 1950, Israel paid the United Nations $54,628 in indemnity for Folke's murder.

The assassination and Israel's failure to punish the culprits tarnished the reputation of the United Nations as an organization purported to stand for peace and human rights. The first secretary-general, Trygve Lie, said, "If the Great Powers accepted that this situation in the Middle East could best be settled by leaving the forces concerned to fight it out amongst themselves, it was quite clear that they would be tacitly admitting that the Security Council and the United Nations was a useless instrument in attempting to preserve peace."

But, as Kati Marton wrote in *A Death in Jerusalem*, "If the United Nations spoke with 'considerable authority' early that summer, by fall its voice was barely above a whisper in Palestine. So muted was the world body's reaction, so lacking in any real sanctions against the Jewish state for its failure to pursue the murderers of the United Nations' mediator, that for Israel, 'world opinion' became an empty phrase." Like most Israelis, David Ben-Gurion harbored great resentment for the U.N., an institution the prime minister derided during a cabinet debate on March 29, 1955, by referring to it as Um-Schmum. (Um is the Hebrew acronym for the agency and schm- is a prefix that signifies contempt.) The utterance still reflects the way in which some Israelis view any international authority.

The plane carrying Folke's coffin took off toward Bromma Airport outside Stockholm, where Estelle was waiting with their two sons and his elderly father, Prince Oscar. The funeral was a major international event, attended by royalty, Trygve Lie, and other distinguished guests. Thousands of mourners lined the streets along which the casket was carried, accompanied by members of the Red Cross and the Boy Scouts, to the Gustav Vasa Church, a beautiful structure that seats 1,200 people, making it one of the largest churches in Stockholm. During the service, a Swedish tenor and one of the leading operatic singers of the 20th century, Jussi Björling, sang "Sweden, Sweden our Homeland." His voice trembled at times as tears streamed down his cheeks, with the final notes fading out into a sob. The *New York Times* eulogized Folke as a "man of integrity."

Folke was buried on his wife's birthday, September 26. She was only 44. It was their son, Bertil, nearly 13 at the time, who first heard the news of his father's death announced on the radio. He called out to his mother. He said he could understand Count Bernadotte being murdered, but not his father. After being informed of her husband's death, Estelle reportedly stated: "It has come as no surprise to me. We had both reckoned with the possibility. Many friends had warned us, but I know he was quietly willing to offer his life for peace."

Few reacted to Folke's death with a more wrenching sorrow, and a greater determination to continue with his legacy, than Ralph Bunche, who became the second chief UN Mediator in Palestine. Just 10 days after the assassination, he released a statement: "The threats and ruthless violence of criminal terrorist bands in Palestine will not be permitted to frustrate the determination of the United Nations to achieve a peaceful adjustment of the Palestine situation." He also described his own feelings about the murders of both Folke and Sérot: "There was irony as well as tragedy in Jerusalem on that fateful day on September 17 when Jewish terrorists struck down those two gallant servants of peace. Just 24 hours before, Count Bernadotte had signed his report to the United Nations, which had accepted without question the existence of the State of Israel and which had strongly urged that the truce in Palestine must be promptly superseded by a permanent settlement. I am certain that I express the views of all when I say that our continuing tribute to Count Bernadotte is to do our utmost to carry on the work for which he laid down his life. We have lost an irreplaceable leader, a man of greatest good will, but his inspiration remains with us."

A few weeks later, Bunche stood before the United Nations. He said Folke was not only his chief, but "a treasured friend." Bunche described him as "an utterly honest and fearless man, completely independent in his thinking, and thoroughly devoted to the effort to bring peace to Palestine. He had no axe to grind, no vested interest to serve. The Mediator . . . strove by trial and error through reason and persuasion, and every other honorable means to find a common ground upon which the conflicting parties might meet."

Whenever Folke traveled as mediator, he ordered the aircraft to be marked with the Red Cross. He explained to Trygve Lie that, as mediator, "I did not wish to appear in any way as a representative of the Swedish Red Cross or any international Red Cross organization, but simply of the Red Cross idea as such. I wanted to emphasize the fact that my mission had a strongly humanitarian background and that I wanted to try to be completely objective and neutral when

I met the various representatives of the conflicting forces." Always, Folke held up the Red Cross as one of the few organizations that could truly have an impact.

In his book *Instead of Arms*, published shortly after his death, Folke wrote about his feelings trying to mediate such an intractable dispute: "Distrust and suspicion between peoples should be overcome. This can only happen by an open and honest exchange of views. These exchanges may become sharp and heated; in any case they serve their purpose if they are characterized by a strong desire for understanding. The weapons used may be sharp — but if they are clean, there are possibilities that the wounds will heal. It is my hope and conviction that the Red Cross will become one of the most efficient organizations which can contribute to the settling of differences of opinion, which, because of the weaknesses and faults in human nature, have always existed between the peoples of the world."

The last few paragraphs of the book were written on July 10, 1948. "As I am dictating these lines, my plane marked with the Red Cross is over the blue Mediterranean. My negotiations are now entering their second phase. I am not pessimistic. It seems to me that the door which both parties have left ajar has opened a little wider. In a few days, I hope to return to Palestine, with the aid of this white plane, to resume contacts with the fascinating leading figures of the Middle East. It is still an open question whether or not I will succeed. I am, however, firmly resolved to try in every way to fulfill the hopes placed in me."

A Legacy of Leadership

Livia Szmuk (now Fränkel) grew up in the 1930s in the city of Sighet in Transylvania, today part of Romania but at the time under Hungarian rule. It was an isolated region, surrounded by the harsh wilderness of the Carpathian Mountains, where 10,500 Jews lived at the start of the Second World War. Elie Wiesel, the noted Holocaust survivor and Nobel Peace Prize winner, also grew up in Sighet.

Livia and her older sister, Hedi, were raised by caring parents. In their close-knit household, life was good. But as it happened in March 1944, when she was only 15, a series of alarming events sent her life careening in a very different direction. First, German authorities ordered her family to turn over all their valuables or else run the risk of execution. Then, they were forced to wear an identifier — a yellow Star of David marked with Jude, the German word for Jew. Livia and her sister were prohibited from attending school. They witnessed the burning of synagogues.

But what does Livia remember most? Hearing Hitler on the radio for the first time.

"One day I heard a voice in German saying that all the Jews of Europe should be extinct," she says. "This was the first time I heard Hitler and he finished all his speeches with the idea that every Jew in Europe should be destroyed. He had talked like this for a while, but it didn't seem like anybody really took him seriously," she adds.

On May 14, 1944, Livia, Hedi, her parents, Wiesel, his family, and all the other Jews of Sighet were deported in cattle cars to a concentration camp. Livia says now that she had no idea at the time where they were going, only that they had to go — and fast. After traveling for three days and two nights, with no food or water, Livia finally arrived at a place called Auschwitz, where the men were separated from the women. Then, she and Hedi were torn apart from their mother. Within hours of arrival, most of the deportees would be gassed.

"My father went off, and I couldn't even say goodbye to him," she recalls.

They never saw each other again. SS officers ordered Livia and her sister to wait in a line on the right and their mother to wait in a line on the left. Panicked, she did not want to let her girls go.

"She tried to drag both of us in her direction, but those SS men were very, very determined," Livia says. "Her last words to us were, 'Take care of each other, children,' which is what we've done."

Later the girls found out that their parents had been murdered, their father on May 17 and their mother a day later, in the gas chambers. At Auschwitz alone, the SS was capable of murdering 6,000 people a day, 180,000 a month. Each one someone's sister, or mother, or father, or brother. Each life leaving a void in someone else's. And that was just one camp.

After six weeks in hell, the sisters were sent to a labor camp in Hamburg. There they slaved away for 10 months before the camp was closed at the end of March 1945. Livia says she was one of the lucky ones: she was tall. Otherwise, she might not have been permitted to be a slave laborer. "Not all 15-year-olds were allowed to live," she says.

Their first taste of freedom came on April 15, when they were extricated from the concentration camp aboard a White Bus. They were liberated and eventually transported to Sweden. The sisters settled there, got married, and — over many decades — enjoyed raising a passel of children and grandchildren. They could have lived out their lives in relative obscurity. But instead, they've made it their mission, every single year since, to tell younger generations about the atrocities they endured during the Second World War. Crisscrossing Europe, they've visited school group after school group after school group so that the Holocaust never fades from the world's memory.

Livia and Hedi haven't been the only ones. Manya Moszkowicz immigrated to the United States after being rescued, marrying a fellow survivor, Joseph Friedman, and raising two children, Gary and Linda. She went on to become a volunteer at the United States Holocaust Memorial Museum in Washington, D.C., and an active member of the museum's Speakers Bureau. Like Livia and Hedi, Manya traveled extensively for decades, sharing her story and giving a voice to the six million who were murdered. In 2008, she told a group of 70 students that she relives her painful experiences so that all those people didn't die in vain. "We have an obligation to them to fight against genocide," she said. "We are trying to convey to you [young people] what happens when hate, prejudice, and disregard for human life prevail."

Manya died in 2013 — a reminder that the number of Holocaust survivors is steadily dwindling. After the war, 90 percent of them were between age 16 and 45. At the time of this writing, the youngest survivors, who were born in the final phase of the war, are approaching 75. Their shared history makes them a tight-knit group. No one else can truly understand what they went through.

On the sunny morning of May 29, 2018, Livia and Hedi — who today live only a few minutes from one another — arrived at the Riksdag, the seat of the Swedish Parliament, a beautiful neoclassical structure in the old part of Stockholm. They were among 50 people invited to attend the unveiling of a bust of Folke Bernadotte. The lovely 30-minute ceremony was held in the presence of Queen Silvia and Crown Princess Victoria, as well as the speaker of the Riksdag, Urban Ahlin. Also in attendance were Folke's son, Bertil; Bertil's wife, Jill; and Folke's grandson, also named Folke.

Afterward, Bertil, Jill, Queen Silvia, and Crown Princess Victoria mingled and made small talk with Livia and Hedi. They know each other well. They've come together at similar events countless times before.

Born in 1935, Bertil married Jill Georgina Rhodes-Maddox in 1981. They have three children and now divide their time between Britain and Sweden. Folke's other surviving son, Folke Jr. — born in 1931 — married Christine Glahns in 1955. They have four children. Between them, the two sons enjoy many grandchildren. Today, Folke Jr. lives with his wife in a middle-class apartment in Uppsala, Sweden, about 44 miles north of the capital. In their living room is a dark-wood side table, on which is prominently featured two large framed photos, one of Folke Jr.'s mother and one of his father.

Like Livia and Hedi, both Bertil and Folke Jr. have granted interviews and given speeches over the years, with an eye to preserving their father's legacy and fighting those who would prefer to forget.

After Folke was assassinated, their mother, Estelle Bernadotte, remained dedicated to his favorite causes for the rest of her life. She continued his Red Cross work, served as president of the Swedish Girl Guides and Scouts Association from 1949 to 1957 and was also involved with UNICEF and the international conservation movement. Later, she helped maintain a home for elderly women in Stockholm and was the president of the Folke Bernadotte Foundation for the aid of cerebral palsy victims. On March 3, 1973, 68-year-old Estelle married Eric Ekstrand, who had been Master of the Household to the late Princess Sibylla, mother of the current king of Sweden, Carl XVI Gustaf, and who was also in charge of administering Estelle's own fortune. The couple settled in Saint-Paul-de-Vence, near Nice, although they continued to spend a lot of time in Sweden. Estelle died May 28, 1984, at the age of 79, after a long illness following hip surgery. Her widower died four years later, in 1988.

In the years after Folke's death, Estelle continued to appear on the royal scene. She was often present for the annual January State Opening of Parliament. Today, while Folke Jr. is rarely seen in royal circles — mostly due to his poor health and inability to travel — Bertil remains a good friend of King Carl Gustaf, who spent his wedding night at Bertil's summer house on the island of Ingarö in the Stockholm archipelago.

In February 2012, Bertil was present at the service of thanksgiving at the Palace Church following the birth of Princess Victoria's first-born child, second to the throne, who was given the same name as his mother, Estelle. No official explanation was given as to why Victoria and her husband, Prince Daniel, would pick the name, which is of French origin and not Swedish, and which does not have any previous royal history. Indeed, the choice completely ignores the tradition to which the names of future monarchs normally adhere. That the princess might be named after Estelle Bernadotte was a surprise to royal-watchers.

In September 2008, media outlets confirmed that — years before his marriage — Folke had a daughter with vaudeville actress Lillie Ericson-Udde (1892–1981). That daughter, Jeanne Birgitta Sofia Kristina Matthiessen (1921–91), was adopted by Carl G.W. Matthiessen when he married Lillie in 1925. Reports say that Lillie and Folke were deeply in love and intended to marry, but Folke's parents were vehemently opposed to the idea of their son marrying an actress. So the two ended their romance. And while Folke apparently provided financially for his daughter, she was never part of his life. Although a dozen or so of Jeanne's descendants are alive today, her parents' relationship is rarely mentioned.

While Folke's surviving sons remain intent on honoring their father's legacy, Heinrich Himmler's two surviving children, the son and daughter he had with mistress Hedwig Potthast — Helge Potthast and Nanette Dorothea Potthast — refuse to speak of their father or of their experiences during and after the war. The son Himmler had with his wife, Margarete Boden, Gerhard von Ahe, died in 2011. Their daughter, Gudrun Burwitz — the only one of Himmler's offspring who was completely loyal to her father until the very end — died on May 24, 2018, at age 88. One item circulated just after her death was a diary entry she wrote at the age of 12 after her father took her to the notorious Dachau concentration camp. "We saw everything we could," she wrote. "We saw the gardening work. We saw the pear trees. We saw all the pictures painted by the prisoners. Marvelous."

Today Bertil Bernadotte has nothing but disdain for Himmler and for any of the Nazis. And all these years later, his annoyance over the lingering criticisms of the work his father performed is palpable. "You don't murder a nice person, so it's easier to write that my father was a mean man or that he did bad things or that he made all kinds of mistakes," Bertil says. "He could have had a much nicer life, but he chose to take on the jobs he did and was very brave to do so. My father and the [rescue workers] drove by night and they had to travel around with explosives going off like popcorn. He did all he could to help others. A great man was killed."

And, according to Bertil, Folke was a humble man. "When I was a boy, he got to his office at the Red Cross by riding there on his bike," he says. "He never allowed us to think of ourselves as really royal, or as more important than anyone else."

Despite several official investigations into his father's assassination, the crime that shocked the world remained officially unsolved until September 12, 1988, when two former guerrillas of an underground Jewish group once led by Yitzhak Shamir admitted to the media that they had killed Folke 40 years prior. This was the first public acknowledgment of the act by members of the Stern Gang. Yehoshua Zeitler, who said he directed the assassination, told Israeli radio that he had decided to speak out because he feared that the UN would again try to coerce Israel into concessions that would endanger its existence. Meshulam Markover said he led the assassination squad that cut off Folke's convoy with a jeep on September 17, 1948. Three guerrillas jumped out, he said, and one, Yehoshua Cohen, who died in 1986, fired the shots that killed the mediator and his French aide. Cohen never publicly confirmed or denied allegations that he was involved in the assassination. But according to David Ben-Gurion biographer Michael Bar-Zohar, Israel's first prime minister had said Cohen had confessed his role.

Although Folke's ideas sparked an uproar in Israel, and outraged many worldwide, today the Swedish count's name is widely associated with the virtues of compromise and commitment to peace. As for the complaint that Folke gave priority to Scandinavian prisoners over Jews in Nazi concentration camps, an examination by Sune Persson, a highly respected political scientist at the University of Gothenburg, concluded that "the accusations against Count Bernadotte . . . to the effect that he refused to save Jews from the concentration camps are obvious lies." Persson listed numerous prominent eyewitnesses on behalf of Folke, including Folke's close friend Hillel Storch, the representative of the World Jewish Congress in Stockholm, who estimated that the White Buses had saved thousands of Jews.

Today, various institutions bear Folke Bernadotte's name. The Folke Bernadotte Memorial Library at Gustavus Adolphus College — a liberal arts institution in Saint Peter, Minnesota, that's rooted in its Swedish heritage — helps prepare students for future leadership roles. The library supports the intellectual life of the college by developing programs, collections, and an engaging physical space that encourage exploration and learning.

On an even grander scale, the Folke Bernadotte Academy (FBA) in Stockholm is a bustling Swedish government agency working for peace, security, and development, and has the overall mission of supporting international crisis management operations. As part of Sweden's national contribution to global security, it strives to improve the lives of people living in conditions of poverty and repression. The agency offers tailor-made training programs in dialogue and mediation, courses on security in the field, and seminars that bring together experts, researchers, and field workers to share knowledge about the best ways to foster peace and prosperity. Believing in partnerships, the FBA cooperates with a wide range of organizations in countries around the world to resolve conflict, fund peace projects, and to promote respect for human rights.

While there's no doubt Folke's mediation efforts in Palestine didn't resolve the conflict, Sven-Eric Söder, director general of FBA, maintains that his work shouldn't be underestimated. The truce he achieved would later form the basis of the armistice agreement for which Ralph Bunche was awarded the Nobel Peace Prize in 1950. Folke talked and listened to all, and his proposals always took into account the views of all sides, even when Folke didn't agree with them.

"His mediation methods were unpretentious and socially competent, and so should be an inspiration for today's peace mediators. There is also cause to look on his deeds with sober reflection, given that this conflict, all these years on, is still far from resolution," Söder says. "Bernadotte drew early attention to the suffering of Palestinian refugees, and his tireless work for their rights led to the foundation of the UN Relief and Works Agency for the Palestine Refugees in the Near East (UNRWA), whose initial task was to support Bernadotte and monitor the truce in Palestine. Both are still in operation, 67 years later, doing important work."

Had he lived, Söder says, the second Bernadotte plan might have been developed and modified into an important basis for conflict resolution between the parties. He believes its assessment of the status of Jerusalem worthy of consideration, as well as Folke's position on the refugee issue.

"Today, more than ever, in light of the worst refugee situation since World War II, we should remember his commitment to those who are forced to leave their homes. Bernadotte's important contribution to peace and security and his tireless humanitarian commitment deserve respect," Söder says. "We can learn from both his achievements and his mistakes as we continue the quest for a peaceful solution."

Ralph Bunche summed it up best when he said the following just after Folke's death: "I am certain that I express the views of all when I say that our continuing tribute to

Count Bernadotte is to do our utmost to carry on the work for which he laid down his life. We have lost an irreplaceable leader, a man of greatest good will, but his inspiration remains with us."

While the Holocaust should always serve as a reminder of the depths to which humanity can sink, it should also be remembered in celebration of the courageous few who set a moral example for the world to follow. Folke Bernadotte negotiated the release of tens of thousands, saving them from the brink of death. Like the evil that surrounded the Second World War, his extraordinary feats should not be allowed to vanish into historical oblivion.

As Livia said on that bright sunny morning in 2018 at the Riksdag in Stockholm, wearing pink lipstick and a sweet smile, "it must never be forgotten."

ACKNOWLEDGMENTS

To say it's difficult to put into words the tales of a life lived so long ago is a gross understatement. It simply can't be done without the help of those who have gone before.

I am indebted to many writers, but most especially Ralph Hewins, who wrote an informative biography, *Count Folke Bernadotte: His Life and Work*, in 1950, and Sune Persson, who wrote *Escape from the Third Reich: Folke Bernadotte and the White Buses*, in 2009. Folke Bernadotte himself wrote of his own experiences in various books that were so useful, including *Last Days of the Reich: The Diary of Count Folke Bernadotte*. *Newsweek* and other news magazines also published remembrances of Folke's rescue mission that were extremely enlightening.

I want to say thank you to Marianne Kihlberg, a senior advisor at the Folke Bernadotte Academy in Stockholm, who so kindly hung out with me in Stockholm and who put me in touch with Folke's two sons, Bertil and Folke Jr., both gracious, accessible, forthcoming, and introspective.

The two of you shared your memories, and insights, and I'll never forget it. I so admire you both, as well as your remarkable father. I would be remiss if I didn't say thank you to the International Committee of the Red Cross, an agency that has sought to ensure protection and assistance for victims of armed conflict since 1863.

Personally, I'd like to thank my longtime literary agent, the supportive bundle of smarts and energy known as Agnes Birnbaum, a woman I'm also proud to call my good friend. Thank you to Jack David, co-publisher and editor. I'm forever grateful for your support and keen interest in all things related to the Second World War. Thanks to everyone who has helped me at ECW Press. What a hands-on, talented bunch! Thank you Peter Norman, one of the best editors I've ever had the pleasure of working with. Thanks also to Aymen Saidane, David Caron, Rachel Ironstone, and Tania Blokhuis.

Thank you to my bosses at AARP, Myrna Blyth and Jodi Bettencourt, for their encouragement. I appreciate it greatly.

Thanks to my girlfriends in Texas, London, Holland, New Jersey (Inwood Avenue!), Connecticut, South Carolina, and elsewhere who bring such laughter and love to my life. Thanks to my aunt Karen; my mother-in-law, Ginger; and my sister, Paula, for always being there for me. To my children: Chris, Ben, and Olivia. You make every day, and everything, better. And I've no doubt you also will make the world a much better place to live in the years ahead. I love you. This would mean very little without you and your father.

Writing a book can be an extremely lonely pursuit. If you don't have a support system, it's not going to work. My support system is one person, Scott Norvell. Without him looking after our three kids, the house, our dog, Pepper — just about everything — I could never have done this. He's also the best editor I've ever known. I still pinch myself almost daily, barely able to believe that I somehow wound up sharing my life with such a perfect partner.

And finally, as always, a word of thanks to my mother, Lois Ruth, the best in the world. She may be long gone but is in my heart and thoughts every single day — and will be for the rest of my life. What I wouldn't give to have you here with me.

To red wine and *Office* reruns, my companions through many a long stretch of research and writing, thank you.

Finally, and most importantly, I draw so much inspiration from the Holocaust survivors who are slowly passing away. It won't be long before there's no one left to tell their story. Children will read about the Holocaust in textbooks or on the Internet. We must ask questions, share their experiences, and most importantly, never forget.

BIBLIOGRAPHY

Begin, Menachem. *The Revolt: Story of the Irgun.* New York: Nash Publishing, 1977.

Bernadotte, Folke. *The Curtain Falls.* New York: Knopf, 1945.

Bernadotte, Folke. *Last Days of the Reich: The Diary of Count Folke Bernadotte, October 1944–May 1945.* South Yorkshire: Frontline, 2009.

Bernadotte, Folke. *Instead of Arms.* London: Hodder and Stoughton, 1949.

Bernadotte, Folke. *To Jerusalem.* London: Hodder and Stoughton, 1951.

Bullock, Alan. *Hitler: A Study in Tyranny.* London: Odhams, 1952. Revised 1964.

Breitman, Richard. *The Architect of Genocide: Himmler and the Final Solution.* New York: Alfred Knopf, 1991.

Delarue, Jacques. *The Gestapo: A History of Horror.* New York: Paragon House, 1987.

Digeorge, Pat. *Liberty Lady: A True Story of Love and Espionage in WWII Sweden*. Vero Beach, FL: Beaver's Spur Publishing, 2016.

Flapan, Simha. *The Birth of Israel: Myths and Realities*. New York: Pantheon Books, 1987.

Friedlander, Saul. *The Years of Extermination: Nazi Germany and the Jews, 1939–1945*. New York: HarperCollins, 2007.

Gilbert, Martin. *Final Journey: The Fate of the Jews in Nazi Europe*. New York: Mayflower Books, 1979.

Hanson, Victor Davis. *The Second World Wars: How the First Global Conflict Was Fought and Won*. New York: Basic Books, 2017.

Hastings, Max. *Armageddon: The Battle For Germany, 1944–1945*. New York: Vintage Books, 2005.

Hewins, Ralph. *Count Folke Bernadotte: His Life and Work*. London: Hutchinson, 1948.

Himmler, Katrin. *The Himmler Brothers: A German Family History*. New York: Macmillan, 2008.

Hirschler, Gertrude. *Menahem Begin, from Freedom Fighter to Statesman*. New York: Shengold, 1979.

Hitler, Adolf. *Mein Kampf*. New York: Reynal and Hitchcock, 1939.

Ilan, Amitzur. *Bernadotte in Palestine, 1948*. New York: St. Martin's Press, 1989.

Kersten, Felix. *The Kersten Memoirs, 1940–1945*. New York: Macmillan, 1957.

Kirk, George. *The Middle East, 1945–1950*. London: 1954.

Kollek, Teddy. *For Jerusalem*. New York: Random House, 1992.

Kurtzman, Dan. *Ben-Gurion, Prophet of Fire*. New York: Simon and Schuster, 1983.

Lanckoronska, Karolina. *Michelangelo in Ravensbrück: One Woman's War Against the Nazis*. Poland: Spoleczny Institute Sydawniczy, 2005.

Levi, Primo: *Survival in Auschwitz: The Nazi Assault on Humanity*. New York: Touchstone, 1996.

Lyon, Gloria Hollander. *Mommy, What's that Number on Your Arm? A-6374: My Holocaust Memoir*. Bloomington, IN: Xlibris, 2016.

Manvell, Roger, and Heinrich Fraenkel. *Heinrich Himmler*. London: Greenhill Books, 1965.

Marton, Kati. *A Death in Jerusalem*. New York: Arcade Publishing, 1996.

Morse, Arthur D. *While Six Million Died: A Chronicle of American Apathy*. New York: Random House, 1968.

Paine, Lauran. *German Military Intelligence in World War II: The Abwehr*. New York: Stein & Day, 1984.

Persson, Sune. *Escape From the Third Reich: The Harrowing True Story of the Largest Rescue Effort Inside Nazi Germany*. New York: Skyhorse Publishing, 2010.

Phayer, Michael. *The Catholic Church and the Holocaust, 1930–1965*. Bloomington, IN: Indiana University Press, 2000.

Rees, Laurence. *Auschwitz: A New History*. New York: PublicAffairs, 2006.

Roland, Paul. *Life in the Third Reich: Daily Life in Nazi Germany, 1933–1945*. London: Arcturus Publishing Limited, 2016.

Schellenberg, Walter. *The Labyrinth: Memoirs.* New York: Harper, 1956.

Schwarz, Ted. *Walking with the Damned: The Shocking Murder of the Man Who Freed 30,000 Prisoners from the Nazis.* New York: Universal Sales and Marketing, 1992.

Speer, Albert. *Inside the Third Reich.* New York: Simon & Schuster, 1997.

Suster, Gerald. *Hitler: The Occult Messiah.* New York: St. Martin's Press, 1981.

Temko, Ned. *To Win or to Die: A Personal Portrait of Menachem Begin.* New York: Morrow, 1987.

Toland, John. *Adolf Hitler.* New York: Ballantine Books, 1981.

Trevor-Roper, Hugh. *The Last Days of Hitler.* New York: Macmillan, 1947.

Urquhart, Brian. *A Life in Peace and War.* New York: Norton, 1987.

Wiesel, Elie. *Night.* New York: Hill & Wang, 2006.

Wykes, Alan. *Himmler.* New York: Ballantine Books, 1972.

Young, Gordon. *Outposts of Peace.* London: Hodder & Stoughton, 1945.

Special assistance was provided by both Bertil Bernadotte and Folke Bernadotte Jr., as well as the Folke Bernadotte Academy and the Swedish Red Cross in Stockholm, and the United States Holocaust Memorial Museum in Washington, D.C.

PHOTO CREDITS

Cover photograph from The National Museum of Denmark, creator: Odense Christoffersen.

Photos 1 and 57 reproduced from *Instead of Arms* by Count Bernadotte, by permission of Folke Bernadotte Jr.

Photos 3, 6, 7, 18, 23, 25, 27, 29, 31, 34, 36, 38, 45, 50, 51, 52, and 53 reproduced from *Count Folke Bernadotte: His Life and Works*, by Ralph Hewins by permission of Folke Bernadotte Jr.

Photos 4, 5, 8, 30, 33, 39, 40, 43, 46, 47, 48, and 54 reproduced from *A Death in Jerusalem: The Assassination by Jewish Extremists of the First Arab/Israeli Peacemaker* by Kati Morton, by permission of Folke Bernadotte Jr.

Photos 32 and 44: "Endpaper" from *A Death in Jerusalem: The Assassination by Jewish Extremists of the First Arab/ Israeli Peacemaker* by Kati Morton, copyright © 1994 by Kati

Photo 16 credited to the Ravensbrück Memorial Museum.

Photo 24 reproduced from Folke Bernadotte by Sune Persson, by permission of Folke Bernadotte Jr.

Photo 35 courtesy of the GPO.